AF316632

INTUITIVELESS
Challenging Your Gut Feeling

Pablo Ponce

Crisp House

Crisp House

Book Layout © 2017 BookDesignTemplates.com
Cover design by hortasar covers

Intuitiveless / Pablo Ponce. -- 1st ed.
ISBN 978-9942-36-674-0 (hardcover)
ISBN 978-9942-36-675-7 (e-book)

To Paola

CONTENTS

INTRODUCTION

This book is about ideas, ideas on how to deal, in an unusual way, with some of the most important problems in life. A journey to discovering a new way to approach some decisions we need to make in life.

There are different approaches to dealing with problems. A lot has been written about the importance of intuitive thinking. Specifically, it has been a trend for companies to consider the importance of hiring people with that creative or intuitive part related to the right side of the brain. Even though the right brain (creativity) and left brain (logic) theory was debunked long ago, it's an interesting way to simplify certain functions of the brain. Each side of the brain is strong in specific purposes even though a healthy brain always uses both parts. They synchronize through the corpus callosum, and each side complements the other.

It seems like employees with logical minds and highly technical skills who make rational decisions are outdated. What's valued right now is not people with high IQs (IQ mainly measures rational intelligence) but those with high emotional intelligence, intuition, and creativity.

One thing companies consider when hiring is finding an employee who is the right fit. Another is his or her personal life decisions. This book basically focuses on the second one.

It seems that the easiest way to make decisions is by instinct. Why? Because you basically don't have to do anything—just wait until the right idea arrives, hopefully at the right time.

This method of making decisions is the one challenged in this book. It seems that intuition is something you learned about when you were a kid. There's usually a disconnect between the concepts of intuition and belief. Beliefs are things that someone taught you, which, in the present moment, feel like they come to your brain by intuition. In reality, a mix of things you've learned give form to your intuition, along with trusting your instincts, similar to the concept of faith in religion. It works for many types of decisions a person must make in life, but for many others, it's definitely not the right approach.

Intuition doesn't have to be seen as common sense. Common sense might be better seen as rational thinking. How do you open a jar? Yes, common sense. How do you develop a car's engine? Neither common sense nor intuition, in the case of the ordinary person, will help, although intuition might work for someone who's a mechanical engineer or has worked with engines for a long time.

Instinctive decisions are popular because they are linked with creativity. On one hand, in a work environment, creativity might be one of the qualities that can't be replaced with automation or artificial intelligence (AI). On the other hand, for logical processes, technology might simply replace and outperform the human mind. One strength of creative minds is that they tend not to focus on details but on the big picture, which in some specific cases is an asset. This way of thinking is the one that will give more value to most organizations.

The reasons we make personal decisions are very different. One topic of this book, which is a sensitive one, is how to decide whether or not to have children. This decision is usually made by intuition, by something inside the future parents that tells them they should procreate. Throughout the book, different thinking processes will be exhibited that might make you decide differently. Maybe after this analysis, some people's decisions will match what their intuition was telling them. That's great—it's like double checking that they are making the right choice. But it's as important for those people whose rational decisions might make them change their minds about having children.

In a personal decision-making situation, instinctive decisions sound like the safest zone to be in. If, for example, you are making a decision that affects your family, there is not much you need to explain. The reason is that you know that x or y is the right choice; you just don't know why. It requires much less effort, and less effort is what humans love.

Even though the focus of this book is personal decisions, these indirectly affect every aspect of a person's life.

Human behavior is the general topic of this book. The scope isn't scientific or technical. To get the right approach, scientific data was researched, but many of these scientific studies were used as support to give form to the ideas and conclusions, not as a central part of the book.

The book takes an original point of view on every topic. Originality is critical, because it adapts to each human; there's not one right formula for everyone. Data is something that shouldn't be ignored. Data is something that should be used to make smart decisions.

Using the same approach, as usually happens, is what makes all humans alike. We shouldn't be the same; we should be original in our own way, always questioning why there are rules that supposedly we should follow, when deep inside us we know nobody ever taught them to us. We might think that our instincts are the dictating some of these decisions, but maybe it's not instincts but rules that have been placed in our brains. Some of these rules have been passed down through generations, and if we think deeply about them, there is a high probability that we have never understood them. There isn't just one reason why we act in an x or y way; there are millions of reasons. And each person is responsible for deciding the best approach for dealing with these actions. If they are useful, interesting, practical, or proven, share them with everyone. That's the way we all grow, from the sharing of knowledge.

The controversial themes presented in this book are the ones in which a logical mind-set is more effective for making decisions. When we use rational thinking, we start focusing on the counterintuitive. This process teaches us to be more critical in our thinking while we are expanding our knowledge.

Controversial topics, such as family, having children, friends, and money are subjects that commonly can't be talked about candidly and openly because they create an awkward atmosphere. When you are reading a book, there is no such awkwardness, so it's a great moment to relax, think, disagree with what you're reading, or be OK with it. It's valid to question everything. Sometimes the opinions that we instinctively disagree with, counterintuitively, are the very ones that make us grow, the ones that bring up the not-so-easy-to-manage emotions. And indeed that is when the moment of truth is revealed, when the mind starts to express every counterargument that enriches us all. The more controversial the argument, the more emotional the reactions it generates.

Dealing with strong emotions is a training ground for our minds and our behaviors, as well as for the ways in which we respond to those feelings. The more frequently we are in the presence of emotions, the better we react to them, and we create a balance between emotions and the rational mind. The more we get in contact with emotions, the more we use our brains to discover different alternatives to every idea that comes up. Frequently, the perfect alternative does not exist, but usually there is a more favorable one. The mix of rational and emotional processes make us think deeply to come up with conclusions that, in many cases, are different from the ones we had minutes or hours before.

There's a general misunderstanding that is constantly covered in this book. Creativity is extremely important, but for this creativity to flow in an optimal way, a rational mind and the hard work behind the search for knowledge are indispensable.

There are many life dilemmas that, due to this common or unoriginal way of thinking, we tend to underrate, and conversely, there are many that we overrate. Let's get through this book to discover what they are.

## CHAPTER ONE

IS FRIENDSHIP OVERRATED?

We've been told that the most important things in life in terms of happiness are family and friends.

Even though there are a lot of studies that come to the conclusion that friendship brings happiness, there is interesting research saying basically "It depends." This is *The Savanna Theory of Happiness*.[1] The concept is that the happiness of individuals is due not only to current environment but also to ancestral environment. This effect is actually stronger in less intelligent individuals than in more intelligent ones. *The Savanna Theory of Happiness* analyzes happiness in terms of ethnicity, population density, habitat, seasonal affective disorder, and the one I'm focusing on here—friendship.

This research points out that, in general, people are happier in an environment with friends. Comparing less intelligent people to those who are more intelligent shows there's an interesting difference. "For the less intelligent individuals (mean IQ of 81.39) frequency of socializing with friends has a significant positive effect on life satisfaction. In contrast, among more intelligent individuals (mean IQ of 115.57) those who socialize more frequently with friends were less satisfied with life than those that socialize with friends less frequently."[2]

It's been said that you don't select your family, but you do select your friends. For that reason, if the feeling is mutual, it must be one of the best things that could happen to you. But is it?

There are some studies saying that social relations increase your happiness, increase your life expectancy, decrease illness, and have several other positive impacts. That might well be true if the friends are well selected. The problem is that we are not good at selecting friends. It's something like a deep feeling; how you select friends is also a feeling that is difficult to explain. You just feel a "click," and something comes from your guts telling you that you can trust and make a connection with someone. (This is one of the times when you should trust your gut feelings.) In some ways, it's like what you feel in a love relationship, but in other ways it's different. It's somehow similar to a friendship connection: someone with whom you have a lot in common whom you can talk with and who keeps you interested. The difference between friendship and a potential couple is that with this last one, you have two possible outcomes:

First, if you don't make enough of a connection, that usually marks the end of the relationship. (It can last three minutes or your entire life.) The second possibility is that you make a romantic connection; if there is chemistry and you have many things in common, then a formal relationship can start. This moment is when there is a significant difference from the situation called friendship. With that couple, the goals tend to be or should be mutual. The good intentions are also mutual because if one has a problem, it's really an issue for both. It affects both as equal participants. That's the reason the relationship is more real than friendship, which differs on this point. When you have a problem, your friends don't necessarily suffer with you; your friends are not affected by your issue, and in the end, they might not care that much. It feels like friendship in many ways is more a competition rather than a mutual love.

When competition exists in any area of your life, you see competitors as the ones in your category: friends, people you relate to in the office or at the sports club, neighbors, and so on. You don't see the top performers in any area as your competitors.

People are always searching desperately for happiness even though they aren't thinking too deeply about how to live it. Few people know the secret road to happiness, for which there's no definitive answer. Many will have their strategies for being happy, and a common way to measure this is how successful they have been in their lives. The problem is determining success in comparison to whom.

In comparison with the people in their category. It's absurd, this way of thinking; it will never lead them to a happy life, but it is the easiest philosophy for an average human being to understand because it is what they are used to seeing. It's not something people think; it's a combination of what they have learned in life from their parents, their friends, school, work, and the media.

People you are intimate with in your life can have a harsh impact on you if you don't know how to deal with them and change your mind about the type of relationship this friendship creates. It could be argued that relationships with friends are healthy when they are not intimate; when you have contact, you are just exchanging ideas that can be mutually beneficial in terms of knowledge, fun, or something similar. The moment you start sharing intimate details is when problems begin. With the sharing of intimate details, the comparison starts. Envy, pain, anxiety, and several other reactions start to emerge at this moment. The more you share, the more vulnerable you become and the more points of comparison you have with that person. That means more suffering.

How about a friend of yours letting it be known that he or she is spending $20,000 on a holiday trip to an exotic place while you are struggling to pay your kid's school tuition? Or a friend purchasing a $1 million house for cash when you are far from being able to purchase a studio? All these types of conversations create awkward feelings in most people, so if these conversations become more frequent, the one with the less fortunate life is going to feel like a loser.

That's why it's healthier to have friends but not to have too deep a relationship as previously suggested. Have someone to share ideas with but not someone with whom your life becomes a competition. Your relationships should be something additional in your life, not the core of your life. The core must be your partner, your kids (if you have them), your passions, and your interests. Friends should be just a complement, like a hobby you engage in sometimes. When the contact is limited, the meetings are very enjoyable. When they are infrequent, they are special like that exotic chocolate you have sometimes—not every day so it loses its appeal and turns into a cholesterol problem.

Schadenfreude, defined as the enjoyment of another's misfortune, is a word that pops up when talking about friendship. Technically, what is the opposite of this word? This opposite doesn't appear in the dictionary, but a close antonym would be *compassion*. That means if someone has a misfortune in his or her life, you will have compassion for that person. Let's find a different word. How about when someone has something great going in his or her life, and you feel a state described by that word. That antonym will be envy. So, in summary:

Schadenfreude: being happy with someone's misfortune

Schadenfreude antonym #1: having compassion for someone's misfortune

Schadenfreude antonym #2: envying someone's success.

Due to the competition that's frequently present in friendship, schadenfreude is a feeling that is experienced by many people. The term appeared in the English dictionary in 1868,[3] so the definition of this feeling has been with us a long time, related to both ways mentioned: being happy when someone is going through a difficult situation and feeling envy when someone is having a great time.

So, knowing that most people have this dark feeling, it's important to know how to deal with it. One way is to meditate, internalize, and try to control your ugly or negative feelings. Is that easy? If someone is a deep Buddhist follower, if they live in a Buddhist temple in Nepal or are enlightened, the concept might be easy to conceive. It is smart not always to select the easiest route, but sometimes it's the most practical way because when it's too difficult, there's a high probability that you end up not dealing with the problem.

The ideal is something almost everybody knows. The point is not just knowing the ideal; it's what is possible for every person to do to deal with it. The ideal for making a lot of money? Easy, just get an undergrad degree and a Harvard

MBA, then start working at Goldman Sachs and stay there for twenty years climbing the corporate ladder. Easy, you'll be rich. Staying slim and fit? It's even easier; just work out around twenty hours a week. A weekday combination of six hours of weight training (focusing on core muscles and legs) in conjunction with six hours of cardio combining the elliptical machine with running, cycling, and swimming. (And replace your running shoes after eight hundred kilometers of use to avoid injury.) On weekends do a long training program, like running twenty kilometers or cycling one hundred kilometers. Do ten to fifteen minutes of stretching daily and rest one day a week. Don't eat any packaged food. A plain vegetarian diet with whole foods is preferable. Very colorful dishes because the more colorful the dish, the greater the variety of nutrients you'll get from it. Don't eat fried food or use oil. If there's a need for oil, use coconut oil which is not consider optimal but is better than other oils. Even better if you always obtain fat from avocado and all types of nuts and seeds. Drink no fewer than twelve glasses of water a day, not the common eight. The not-proven eight glasses are for the lazy guys; remember, you'll be working out twenty hours a week, so you'll need much more water. No sugar added to anything and some caffeine but not much, around three cups of coffee a day, and it's better if none after 2 p.m. so you can have your eight hours of sleep each day in a very silent, dark room (with high-quality blackout drapes) and with an optimal temperature between 15.5 and 19.4 degrees Celsius.[4] Take a ten to twenty-minute nap each afternoon to boost your energy, as Daniel Pink says in his book *When,*[5] it's better to have a coffee and immediately take the twenty-minute nap, because the caffeine takes twenty-five minutes to give you an energy boost, so when you get up from the nap, you'll be more alert.

By the way, there's even more. Run two marathons a year or one iron man with great training with a personal trainer with expert knowledge, and repeat these races every year, aiming to improve your personal time by 5 percent each year. Get some fifteen minutes of sun without sunblock (not at noon when the sun is too strong) so you can have your daily dose of vitamin D. For the rest of the day, always use sunblock. Take some additional vitamins to compensate for the ones you are not getting due to being a vegetarian. These are mainly B12, zinc, and iron. Don't drink, smoke, or take drugs. Try to live near your work to avoid commuting stress. Work seated in a Herman Miller Aeron chair so your back won't hurt. Take regular breaks (vacations) if you can; a week's vacation every quarter to relieve stress. Get relaxation massages once every quarter. Get a complete medical checkup every year, so if anything is wrong with you, you'll catch it at an early stage, not when it's too late.

Save at least 30 percent of your net salary, invest monthly in a low-cost index fund or ETF, and avoid stock speculation at all costs so you can follow Warren Buffett's first and second rules: First, never lose money, and second, never forget rule number 1.[6] Make a yearly budget and stick to it, knowing where every penny that you spend goes. Spend the budget assigned to "wants" mostly on experiences rather than things. Never stop learning. Read a book every week and avoid TV. Think fast and speak slow. Speak less; listen more. Find true love and stick with her or him for the rest of your life. One last thing; don't forget to be nice to people and animals.

The ideal is easy to know. Everyone can give you the ideal for everything. The 10,000-hour rule, popularized by Malcom Gladwell in his book *Outliers*,[7] is a great concept as a starting point, even though it was superseded by *The Click Moment*.[8] If you follow this rule from the age of six, and spend 10,000 hours, you'll be great at playing the violin, chess, or anything you like. Frans Johansson, the author of *The Click Moment*, says that it only works in circumstances with stable structures where the rules never change, as in classical music and tennis. In other fields the rule is not a great predictor of success.

The problem is that the ideal is worth almost nothing. The ideal is interesting to know so you can analyze how much you can adapt that ideal to your current life or use it for goal-setting purposes. It's also useful for those top performers of the world, who in reality are very scarce. In real life, for common people, it is not very useful. The ideals are so tough for most people, they end up following half of what the ideal is. That's why the personal second best is a great concept. If the ideal is too complicated, there is another one that is perhaps not as good but is better than nothing and much more attainable than the "perfect" one. It's much more useful for most of the population, and that is the one that's more important to know.

Usually there are different ways to deal with a problem. For example, if a person wants to lose weight, there are several ways. They can go on a diet, increase their workout time, change the type of workout they do, have a surgical procedure to reduce their stomach size, or due a combination of these or several other things. But which is the correct one? The correct one can be different for each person. If one person hates working out or can't perform aerobic exercise because their knee is not working well, maybe those are discarded, and the conclusion is reached that just the diet is the ideal. If a diet is too tough because someone is very anxious, maybe the surgical option is ideal. If the person loves sports, but the sport he or she loves is playing darts, and it's the only sport he or she plays, it wouldn't be easy to lose weight. So in this case maybe surgery is better. The point here is that there is no absolute or an ideal answer. The correct answer is what is best for that specific person. Most people might say the ideal is a balanced diet with regular exercise. But maybe that ideal is impossible for a particular person. Maybe spending $15,000 on a surgical procedure is more attainable for that physical and personality type. It might be as simple as that.

Taking all these ideas as a reference, someone can say that the ideal way to liberate your mind of Schadenfreude is simply by not having it. To resist that ugly feeling that comes to your mind and just have pure thoughts. Convert that feeling into compassion or, if someone is having great success and you're not, avoid feeling envy. As with the diet example, this recommendation is not feasible for every person. There might be some other "not ideal" options that are much easier to obtain. A great way to control these obsessive feelings is to avoid that intimate relationship. The ideal way to avoid these types of feelings is having few but good interactions with deep conversations; deep in the sense of serious and generic, not personal. Deep in the way that makes you think and grow, not in a way that makes you compare yourself to the other person, which can rate you as a winner or a loser.

Friendship can be compared to a useless hobby. There are hobbies that make you grow; others make you lose time. Some make you more intelligent; some make you dumber. Some make you healthier and stronger, some make you sick and weak, some make you talented or expert in a specific area, and others don't.

Many humans like to spend their spare time or all the time doing simple things, things that don't challenge their thinking or any specific ability. That's why it is much more common to see some guys watching TV after work instead of learning to play the violin. Or even worse, multitasking, such as watching TV while scrolling Facebook. It's easier than just watching TV because you don't need to pay as much attention to it. Paying attention makes you tired, and that's what many people are avoiding. Even though the brain is the organ in the body that burns the most calories, only a few calories are burned through thinking.[9]

Most people like to do easy things. Things that make them think the least. Thinking all day is exhausting, and humans naturally try to avoid feeling tired. Humans instinctively avoid pain, and exhaustion is pain. The more you think, the easier it is to get frustrated because you figure out that there are more links to what you want to reach that you need to find. Thinking about anything you want to create, it's easy to get frustrated. Creation requires inspiration, knowledge, focus, research, and something crucial: time. Most humans want to differentiate themselves from others. They want to create even though they might not know what to create and end up in the middle of the road of creation because the road itself is not easy. Most end up taking the easy road, which doesn't take them to those dreamed goals—only a life without sacrifice full of disappointments. This idea takes them to the root of why people like social life and like to be in touch with friends.

Hanging out with friends and having a social life is taking the easy road. It's the simpler way to kill time doing something that is not going to change the world or even one person's life. People need challenges to do impressive things, and hanging out with friends won't challenge anyone—it is just the comfort zone. You do need some qualities like social skills to hang out with friends or to get to know new people. For many it is not as easy as it is for others. But somehow every single human ends up having a group of friends. Statistical data reveal that for Americans the number of friends per person varies from 7.4 to 9.6—7.4 for people with earnings of more than $75,000 a year, and 9.6 for those earning less than $30,000. The number for those who earn $30,000 to $40,000 is 8.0, and in the range of $40,000 to $75,000, it is 8.2.[10]

One interesting conclusion in another study is that 9 percent of American adults responded that they did not have any good friends to whom they feel close.[11] One of the reasons people have so few friends might be that they value the quality of the friends rather than quantity.[12] This is about friends who are different than intimate relations. Regarding intimate relations, who include your partner, family, and friends, it's been said that a human can maintain only five intimate relations at once.[13] If you have a partner (husband, wife, girlfriend, boyfriend), there is space for only four more people in your life at this level. The main reason is that relationships demand time and mental effort, and five is the capacity of humans.[14] This number is much smaller than you might expect. Imagine living that easy life, avoiding pain through thinking and creating things, and people can only handle five intimate relations; now imagine what it would be like for a person who really uses time wisely.

The more time you spend on your social life, the less you create, mainly because to create something you need two basic ingredients: focus and time. Being too social makes you feel as though you're living an unfulfilled life because you are not using your time wisely. Besides that, if you are in the group of intelligent people quoted in *The Savanna Theory of Happiness*, you'll be less happy. You go through life as a spectator, not as a creator, which isn't the best choice. What do you think is better, watching a football game or being a football player? Watching a movie or being an actor in it? Reading economic news or being the Fed chairman? It sounds like it is unanimous that being the protagonist is better than being a spectator (unless you were in the ancient Roman circus).

The problem is that being a protagonist requires thinking, creation, time, and focus, hardly possible with the distraction of social life. That social distraction will help you up to the point that you can have the network necessary to gain an important position. The problem is that you can't stay in that position without the right talent and knowledge. No network on earth will place you as the Fed chairman if you don't have a tremendous talent for that.

Might this be the reason that more intelligent individuals feel more satisfied in life with less contact with friends? Maybe it's because the more intelligent people are, the more they understand that in life, they should search for meaning and creation. Everything is connected, so they feel less satisfaction in friendship because they think they might be losing time to develop the things that they really care about in life. Elements that really fulfill their dreams and consequently give them the time they need to focus on what gives them the most satisfaction.

Carl Jung, the famous Swiss psychiatrist, used to retreat to a second home he had on Lake Zurich for several months each year. He went alone and had no contact with the outside world.

He traveled there with the idea of focusing on his work and creating without any disturbances. This is nothing new. It's a common practice among influential leaders and thinkers, such as Bill Gates, to take some weeks off each year to focus and think.

There is another way besides going on retreat every year. Most successful executives and leaders say that spending a lot of time on your work and ideas is the best way to reach a goal. The idea is not the main component of this success. What is really important is working on it. That's what really makes the difference. It is not important to think about a theme to write a book. The difficult part is writing it. Neither is it the difficult part to have an idea about a specific technological advance; the difficult part is to develop it, and the even more difficult part is to create the ideal marketing strategy so that the product is successful. Ideas and creations flow by dedicating an immense amount of time and focus. Without it, it is very difficult indeed to succeed.

But let us not lose focus. It's not that a person shouldn't have friends, but friends should be the ones who give you an impulse to be a better you, in any field. Friends who make you think so you can use that extra knowledge in a positive way to reach your goals. Finding these friends is not an easy task. And at the end of the day, that might be one of the reasons Americans report having about eight friends and not eighty.

Friends are overrated in part because they take time and focus away from your life, time that could be used to develop something that gives meaning to your life and maybe to the world. Friends also fill your brain with bad decisions because you enter into a foolish, nonsensical competition that makes you spend money and time unwisely. The positive impact of friendship is totally void when analyzed the negative aspects.

Life is a constant trade-off. You lose something when you decide on one option. If you choose the right friends and manage them correctly, it can be a gain, but many times, this is not the case. If you decide to sacrifice time a focus it should be for gaining something in your life. One of the cons of friendship is the feelings of schadenfreude and envy. It's a feeling that makes people's lives miserable. In these common cases, it's better not to make friendship a priority in your life. There is scientific evidence that, at least for intelligent people, socializing makes them unhappier. One thing that diminishes when socializing is spending time and focus that could be more useful if spent on creating things and expanding knowledge. It might be intuitive that friends bring you happiness, but the logical part of it is that to fulfill your goals in life, you need time to focus. If you don't develop anything, you pass your life as a spectator, not as a protagonist. Life is definitely better being a protagonist.

Is that maybe the reason that the most intelligent people prefer to be alone?

Life is short, and you should choose wisely.

DECIDE WHAT TO PURCHASE

Have you ever thought that having children is really like purchasing something? It might not be the same as buying a product, but it basically is. Some people will say that you're selfish and ignorant just to propose that idea. The thing is that, technically you are buying something you should take care of; in other words, it needs maintenance.

Yes, having a child involves feelings, and buying a jacket doesn't somehow. The thing is that a purchase is something we spend money on, which now becomes part of our equity, our possessions, or our experiences. What dictates if something is considered a purchase is not feelings.

Purchases can be divided in two categories: investments and expenses.

Investments are something you spend your money on, and at the end of a certain period, you have a profit or loss: for example, stocks, real estate, gold, art, and many other items. At the end of the period, you can earn a lot, earn something, lose something, or you can lose everything. That's how it works.

On the other hand, expenses involve money that you use for the following purposes: eating, entertainment, clothing, transportation, and others. You can't take these categories literally because, for example, an athlete spending a lot on what he or she eats is an investment, and for an executive, clothing can be an investment to climb the corporate ladder because his image is important, and so on.

Keeping these two categories in mind, which does having children most probably fit into? If you have a child like tennis player Serena Williams, it is an investment. That's what happened to her father, who dedicated his life to making her what she is. This case is an exception to what a child is usually considered, financially speaking. In most cases, he or she will be considered an expense. Why?

Raising a child will cost you $233,000[15] for the first eighteen years of his or her life if you give him or her a middle-class lifestyle. If you plan to give him or her a high-class lifestyle, it'll be $372,000.[16] Keep in mind that is up to eighteen years of age, so those figures don't include college tuition and expenses.

We could go deeper into the math of raising a child, but that is not the point here. On average people don't have just one child. Depending on which country you want to consider, most couples have two kids. (In 2015 the average number of kids per woman worldwide was 2.4.)[17]

People have children because of a deep feeling. Some people call it biological, or say it's because it's natural for every human, or that you should leave a legacy. The last thing people analyze is whether it is a good idea financially, if it's something they can afford, or what's going to be the payment plan for that expense.

The formal process when you want to purchase something and don't have the money is to go to a bank. You ask for credit, and they analyze your equity, earnings, and debts, among other things. For instance, if you ask for $200,000, and it is above the range of what you can easily pay, the credit is simply denied. The bank uses software that details many variables of your profile, and that software gives them a recommendation. It is not just simple computing because, obviously, there are human criteria involved. But after a quick analysis, it's easy to know the answer. It's a scorecard where you pass or you don't.

How about if we used this software to see if we are approved to have a child? Lots of us would fail. The point is that no one is controlling whether you are making a smart choice, financially speaking. People think that because this specific expense is related to a feeling, they have the right to it, and the money somehow will come. Yet in most cases, this doesn't happen.

To know if people have made a good or a bad decision, just take a glance at the 2017 wealth report by Credit Suisse:[18]

- 70 percent of the world's population (adults) has a net worth of less than $10,000.
- With $77,000 of net worth, you are in the top 10 percent of the world's population (adults).
- With $770,000 of net worth, you are in the top 1 percent of the world's population (adults).
- Switzerland net worth (median wealth) per adult: $229,000, first in the world.
- United States net worth (median wealth) per adult: $55,000, twenty-first position in the world.

Just do some simple analysis of this data. Switzerland is the number one–ranked country in net worth per capita, and it's the same amount it costs to raise a child. In the United States, the average net worth is more than four times the median wealth to raise a child.

It seems incomprehensible the way people think and decide. Financial analysis is not undertaken for such important decisions. On the other hand, one of the most important decisions, whether or not to have a child which is up to you, is not made through a deep analysis. If you don't have the money and want to spend $15,000 to remodel your kitchen, you get the urge to go into deep analysis, but not for committing $233,000 to raising a child.

There's a great difference between spending money on having a child and on anything else. If you make the wrong decision about an investment—buying the wrong stock, for example— you can just sell it and assume the loss. That's the end of the problem. If the investment were a condo you purchased and ended up not liking for some reason, you could sell it—maybe for a profit or maybe for a loss. That's also the end of the problem.

If you make the wrong decision in terms of an expense rather than an investment—for example, you had an impulse to purchase a very expensive bag—maybe you regret it later, and you lose the amount you paid for it, or you sell it on eBay for a loss. But how about the children?

You can't return the children; you can't sell them back or simply decide not to take care of them. If it was the wrong decision, you'll have it with you for not less than eighteen years, and some parents would even say you'll have that worry for the rest of your life.

There is a more complex problem about that expense. Once you decide to have one child, if you don't have the experience of doing it, you can't be sure how it feels. Compare it with a meal you're planning to eat out. How about if you go to a fancy restaurant, and you have never tried rabbit? You think, "OK, let's try it." You know that you can't return that dish because that's the intrinsic rule in any restaurant. You can return it if there is something wrong with the dish, but not because you just don't like the type of dish you ordered. You wait the usual twenty minutes, the waiter puts the rabbit on your table, and you have the first piece of it. Suddenly you realize that rabbit is not your type of food.

In this case the point about having children is that you can't return them. The difference is that in the case of the rabbit, you have two choices: leave the restaurant starving or wait another twenty minutes while the waiter brings you a different meal. In either case, you have just lost perhaps twenty dollars' worth of rabbit.

This point is just to illustrate how critical the decision is. Even when the possible loss is minor, you think a lot before doing it. Nobody wants to show up in a pink tuxedo to a black-tie event.

How about having a child and figuring out later that kids are not for you? Besides that first discovery you have, you also conclude that you don't have enough money to take care of your child.

As is said in the movie *Parenthood*, "You need a license to buy a dog or drive a car. Hell, you need a license to catch a fish! But they'll let any butt-reaming asshole be a father." [19] Aside from the comic part, it makes sense. Apart from the idea of using the financial software banks use to decide whether or not you should have a child, there are several institutions that regulate and decide if you are allowed to do a specific thing, such as driving a car. The ironic part is that nobody analyzes whether or not you are capable of raising a child. Maybe there's an opportunity for developing something like a psychological test in which the scorecard will tell you how capable you are of raising a child. Combine that with the financial software, and you are ready to make the most important decision of your life.

At this moment in the chapter you must be thinking, "Well, kids make their parents so happy that the expense is worth it, despite the risk of not having enough money. They can figure that out later." If that's the case, your intuition is wrong. It is not something that makes most of the parents extremely happy. In the upcoming chapters, you can see data that supports this.

Purchasing things should definitely be a programmed activity. It should be planned. It may sound like you can have all the numbers in your head and make every decision just because it sounds like a good alternative for your life. The problem is that you can't rely on your instincts for this. Sadly, it doesn't work that way.

## CHAPTER THREE

ARE KIDS OVERRATED?

In certain ways the experience with kids takes you to the same issues as having friends. The pros and cons of having kids have been talked about a lot. There are people who believe that having a child is almost the main part of their existence, that biologically we are meant to procreate and leave a legacy. There is in some cases a small part of us that thinks that none of this is true and that every human has their own ability to decide what is better for their personal well-being.

It's been concluded, based on analysis, that a lot of people say they would have a feeling of emptiness in their lives if they had decided not to have children. When they have children, they say that they couldn't imagine how life would be without them, a totally nonsensical life.

In these cases, people are already parents. Let's analyze each of these situations. First, the "emptiness" that not having children would cause you. When you were single, young, and full of life, did you feel that emptiness of not being a parent? Did you have a bad time because you didn't have someone to take care of? Were you constantly depressed, bored, and without goals or aspirations in your life? In general this is not the case, and if there are some young people who do feel those symptoms, it is not because they don't have children; it's for other reasons. The least of the problems of young people feeling depression, boredom, and lack of goals is not having kids.

So why is there a time in life when you are very fulfilled and happy, and suddenly you feel that your life doesn't make sense if you don't have a kid? What changes? If you don't own a house on a beach when you're thirty, why would life make less sense if you didn't own that house in your forties?

It's clear that tastes in life evolve or simply change. Not really evolve, because to evolve means that something changes for good, and that's not always the case. In terms of tastes, there's no good or bad; it's just as it is.

Someone could challenge this argument about the children or the house on the beach. "Yes, in your late twenties, the last thing you think of is a house on the beach when you are maybe focusing on how to get into graduate school and pay for your master's degree." Then in your forties you have new things to worry about, and maybe there's no sense in living without a house on the beach!" Well, yes. Tastes change, but you also adapt to what is reachable in your life. You can't say, "Life is nonsense without winning a Nobel Prize," or "Life is nonsense without owning a private jet." If you think like that, you're going to be miserable. Those two examples are almost impossible to attain statistically speaking. But how about "Life is nonsense if I can't run every day," or "Life is nonsense if I can't eat chocolate anymore." These are examples of things you used to like, but under new circumstances, you can't continue with them, and you need to adapt. In the end people end up adapting to those types of things, creating new habits and ditching old ones. These last habits are those you ditch by obligation or because, even though you like them, you think your life will be better without them. That's why you push to leave them for good.

After understanding these examples as a background for the "having children" analysis, let's compare matters:

1. Children as something (almost) impossible to acquire: You can have a kid without any difficulty unless you or your partner are not fertile or you are a same-sex couple. Apart from that, you can have kids. Being physically capable of having kids doesn't cancel the fact that, for many couples, it is almost impossible to raise kids without lots of sacrifices, and it is really difficult taking care of all the costs related to it. On average raising a child is going to leave you with very little money for your retirement or your day-to-day comforts of life. Additionally, it leaves you with no extra time to develop your ideas and creations as mentioned before. These are the ones that require a lot of free time, which is so difficult to find while raising a child.

2. Having children because you think that in the future you will not get used to a life without kids: This is related to the chocolate and running examples previously mentioned. You reach a certain age when you say, "My life doesn't make sense without kids," but the point here is that, when you are young, you have no interest at all at that moment in being a parent. Then you get older, and you acquire

the taste for children but you had decide not to have them. There's a high possibility that you're going to adapt to a life without a child. A child is not something indispensable in life, like having food and shelter every day.

It's like a hobby you are not doing. It's like you love playing golf every day, but for whatever reason, you can't anymore. Even though you might love golf, you end up adapting to a life without golf and, besides adapting, enjoying a life without golf. It's even less painful than a hobby that you are not participating in. In the case of the hobby that you love, it means you once were into it, and it takes time to develop a love for it. In the case of not having children, you haven't had that experience. You never developed a love for it. It's like you can't play football anymore, but you never played it. Will it hurt? Or it can be like a dream that you never tried, so what part would you deeply miss? It's like regretting you'll never in your life land on the moon. Maybe the idea of someday being an astronaut attracted you, but you are not going to have a painful and depressing life because you'll never land on the moon.

You don't need to get everything you dreamed of or travel everywhere you've always wanted to be fulfilled in life. In life there are millions of options, and it's totally acceptable and understandable that you don't need to fulfill every wish to be happy and satisfied. More than that, the pleasure in life is attained by selecting wisely. In many areas a wise selection of roads is what fulfills you. If you can have anything you want, life will be boring. The psychological reward is due to that wise selection. That is the game of life. The idea is taking advantage of all the opportunities that life gives you and to flow with them.

There are many dreams that are not really what you want. In many cases these are only temporary dreams. Think about how much your dreams have changed in your lifetime. Maybe there are some that are still the same, but there are some that have changed. They change with your tastes, with your age, with the unexpected turns that life has given you. Those unexpected changes also create changes in your dreams, purposes, and tastes. That's why you don't have to attach yourself to dreams—at least not to all of them.

It's important to clarify which dreams still work for you. There are some dreams that might have been valid at a certain age, but you already passed that age and didn't accomplish them. So you must go on and find other that better fit your actual way of thinking. Maybe when you were young, you were passionate about going to a specific university. But when time passed and you didn't get into the one you wanted, you went to a different one; at that moment that dream was gone. That dream is not valid anymore because it is impossible to attain. So usually at that moment you start creating new dreams. Even when you end up going to the university you always dreamed of, after four years, you get your degree, and the dream is also gone. You can achieve your dream but either way, you should move on to a different dream.

Dreams are better when they are not that specific. The ideal is the sensation or the concept that you are searching while trying to fulfill that dream. Putting a dream in such a precise way drastically increases the possibility of not reaching it. For example, imagine that one of your dreams is to gain work experience around the globe. If the dream is as specific as "I would love to work at Colgate-Palmolive's headquarters at 300 Park Avenue in New York City," "I would like to get into Stanford's undergrad program," "I would like to be Victoria's Secret model" or "I would like to be accepted into the astronaut program at NASA"… well, in that case you'll be setting the bar so high that the probability of not reaching the goal is very great indeed. The Stanford acceptance rate is 4.69 percent.[20] If you want a NASA spot, there were 18,300 applicants for only 14 slots in the 2017 class; that's a 0.08 percent acceptance rate.[21] How about being a Victoria's Secret angel? Good luck with that dream. According to Victoria's Secret chief marketing officer Edward Razek, fewer than one hundred women in the world have the potential to be a Victoria's Secret model.[22]

There are some studies of what parents think about having kids. Some are fulfilled, and some are not. It is not math. There are people who are happy with the choice, and there are people who are not. The point of all this explanation of the doubts people have about choosing not to have children is to defend the point that having kids will probably make your life worse.

Why select something that you have never tried, that delivers no returns, that is going to consume most of your money and most of your time? Will it make life better? The element of time is the key. It will use time that you really need to focus on creations, on developing something in your life that will allow you to fulfill your dreams.

Let's visualize a typical love story. There is the usual type of couple. They've been in a relationship for a few years, and they decide that it is time to get married, due to love or custom. Once they get married, they spend around two years traveling, doing a lot of things they always wanted to do and feel there is a window of opportunity to do at that stage because, in the future, when kids arrive, things are going to be different (for the better, supposedly). Then they start to get bored with the same type of activities, and they think it's time to make a change in their lives. They don't feel the former sparks anymore, so a child apparently will bring that emotion that they're missing back to life. Then the kid arrives, but this type of couple is one that gets bored with things. So who guarantees that after a couple of years, when the novelty has worn off, the same bored feeling won't arise again? Bad news for them if that comes; there is nothing they can do. They'll stick with it for life (at least for eighteen years, the formative years of their child).

People tend to consider having children their dream. But in the end, it doesn't end up being a smart choice. In this case it is not a matter of tastes as much as a matter of choices. It is different because with any other choice, you usually select from things you have tried before. Do you want to eat sushi or pizza? Do you want to go to the beach or skiing? Do you want to read fiction or nonfiction? Do you want to purchase Zara or Louis Vuitton? In all these cases the possibility of frustration with the decision made is minimal because you clearly know the pros and cons of each choice. With kids you are selecting something without knowing anything or knowing too little about how it will be.

There is a similar example that people try that doesn't necessarily take them to success. This is when you select your career when you enter college. This is one of the toughest choices everyone has in life. This choice is extremely difficult for most people. There are few who since age four knew what they wanted to do once they got older but not the majority. That's the same reason people should think carefully the moment they decide to have kids. It's tough because you are choosing something critical that is going to define your future forever, and you'll decide without having experienced it and without deeply knowing what it is about. Research shows that 80 percent of students end up changing their major at least once.[23] That is part of the proof that people need to experience something before deciding.

There are several things that you decide before trying, but here the difference is that they are not critical in your life. For example, you purchase your first BMW even though it costs you a lot of money, and then after driving it, you realize that you don't like it. Well, in that case, you sell it, only losing a few thousand dollars. You end up going to Barcelona for the first time because it looks amazing in photos. Once there, you don't like it that much. In that case you just adjust your itinerary and go somewhere else. These are like the example above about college careers; the 80 percent who changes their major end up losing time and money, nothing else. They even win some new knowledge from the career they drop.

How about recreational drugs? This is something some people decide to try without knowing what it's going to be like. They clearly hear from the media, papers, analysis, and reports that taking drugs will destroy their lives (not including prescribed drugs as marihuana, which is now legal in some countries and US states). Why are people still trying them? Well, there are large studies about why people fall into drugs, and that's not a point to speak of at length here.

The comparison here is having kids, selecting a career, and deciding whether or not to take drugs for the first time. These decisions have one thing in common: people don't know if they are going to like them. There are differences, as kids can be a pleasure in life, and drugs can destroy your life. It's clear that there are a lot of differences, but focusing on the unknown outcome of liking something or not is the point.

Many drugs are highly addictive, some more than others. Considering the rankings in terms of dependence on the drug, not including legal recreational drugs like tobacco (nicotine) or alcohol, which usually rank high on the lists. There are several rankings that place different drugs as being more dangerous in terms of dependency. According to experts the most dangerous are crystal meth, heroin, and crack cocaine.[24]

The media have been scaring everybody by emphasizing the risk of drug dependency. Drugs not only bring health issues for the user but also social problems. That's why in general there's a lot of discussion about which strategies are optimal for avoiding drug use, the role of the police, and possible legalization, among others.

The highly addictive crystal meth that makes us all nervous just to imagine was researched for years, and the conclusions were presented in the study "*Methamphetamine: Fact vs. Fiction and Lessons from the Crack Hysteria*"[25] by Carl L. Hart, Joanne Csete, and Don Habibi. According to the *National Survey on Drug and Health* (NSDUH), 96 percent of people who have tried the drug have not consumed it in the last month. In a lifetime, fewer than 15 percent of people who try it become addicted. That's the fact.

Keeping this data in mind, in the case of this, the most dangerous drug in the world, even if you try it, there is an 85 percent chance that you can easily drop it if you don't like it.

Getting back to the original point, how about in the case of children?

It may sound like we all need to have children because it is human instinct. It's difficult to make a rule like "Everybody should have children" when it involves a matter of taste. People fear feeling regret in the future if they decide not to have them. Chances are that they'll be fine. It's not logic regretting (in a painful way), not having something that they never had the time to develop love to it. Something they've never tried. Intuition doesn't work well here, in the same way it doesn't work for students selecting their majors in college.

Having kids is a difficult decision because you must decide without knowing if you'll like the outcome. Besides that, kids are "no return"; that's the main problem. It's the only experience that if you don't like it, there is nothing you can do about it. Do people really think about this? Even Mike Tyson's face tattoo can be removed.

## CHAPTER FOUR

KIDS AS THE EASIEST PATH

People tend to prefer a life with kids for several reasons. The main one is that the possibility of not having them does not exist in most people's minds. Among the many reasons people may decide to have them, there is one that is not usually analyzed. This is, because it is the easiest path to take.

Why would it be the easiest path when it is a great responsibility to raise a child, requiring a lot of time, money, stress, and making them the number one priority in your life. The stress it creates is very great while trying to raise them to be intelligent, healthy, useful to society, and responsible. Ensuring they reach a certain age when they will not need their parents as a means of survival but more as friends, companions, or loved ones is an everyday worry. In general terms it looks like it is not the easiest path.

One constant worry in a human being's life is what to do with that life. Which path to follow. Deciding how they are going to spend their time, money, and energy while being happy and fulfilled is not an easy task. For most people it takes decades to realize this, and many don't realize it in their lifetime. They die without knowing it. There are just a minority who, since they were young, knew what fulfilled them and how they wanted to spend the rest of their lives.

Choosing a life with children relieves the worry of searching for what to do with your life. Children represent such a large amount of time and money that they become a very useful excuse for not searching anything anymore. This happens mostly to women because they dedicate more of their time to their children. They dedicate most of their time to the process of upbringing for several years. They justify themselves for not searching for a mission in their lives, saying that their passion, mission, and reason to live is their kids. For some once they have kids, they don't have to think about that mission. It relieves the pressure of, for example, climbing the corporate ladder, creating a business project, being an exceptional athlete, or discovering the cure for some terrible illness. You can justify that you are not in that search because your project is to raise a child. Even if you still have a job, it's secondary. Your child is the priority. That is the easiest road because society totally accepts that type of mission, it's considered a noble mission in life, and people get comfortable with it and stay in that comfort zone. In the end a parent might feel that he or she could have done many things in life at which they could have excelled, but because they decided to get involved in a "child project," they didn't have time to develop the abilities needed to reach that goal. The worst part is that they justify themselves, and even if they don't mind what other people think, they also justify themselves by saying that parents have a great responsibility, and anything is good for the sake of their child.

There are some reasons why it's the easiest road. Humans in general have an average life. That is what the word means.

The average is something that most of a certain group are, do, or have. Being exceptional by definition is not being average. Being exceptional is not a common quality in humans. These are the outliers that Malcom Gladwell dedicated a complete book to.[26]

When someone has kids, most probably these kids will end up being average. When someone is average, it is difficult to measure their success. A great part of how a parent measures their success is through measuring how successful their kids are. While it is almost impossible to measure in an objective way how successful average kids are, parents feel a relief of not having failed in life. In that case they don't feel accountable for their success anymore. Because they can't measure their kids' success, they lie to themselves, feeling they have reached success in life. The way of measuring most humans is subjectively: "Oh, he finished college." "He's not on drugs." "He has a family and is very responsibly taking care of them." "He purchased a house." None of those ways of measuring success are objective. Why is someone successful because he puts a down payment on a house, even though he still owes the bank 90 percent of the cost? Having a family as an example of success, even though a man doesn't love his wife, and his kids are unbearable? Finishing college is being successful, even though that college is the worst in the country?

It is different when you raise a child, and he or she ends up being an outlier. You can measure the success of many outliers in an objective way. In that case the parents can feel they were successful raising their child. If the kid won a gold medal in the Olympic games? Yes, that is objective success because there is an institution rating whether someone if someone is good in a specific activity or not. If someone were to reach the

CEO position in a Fortune 500 company? That's definitely a measure of success. There are thousands of great candidates for a position like that, and he or she was the one chosen for it. If the kid got a Nobel Prize, yes, that's success and that is objective.

When someone decides to take a path in life that doesn't involve having kids, they and others can rate their lives very differently. The goals turn out to be more objectively measurable than the subjective way that measures someone's life through their kids' success. If someone decides to be a swimmer, for example, competing in the fifty-meter freestyle men's category, their personal time should be no more than twenty-three seconds. If it is not, they are simply not in the top tier of the big leagues. That's it. If you have the correct time, you can win; if you don't have it, you lose. Translating this in terms of success, if your time is twenty-four seconds in fifty-meter freestyle, you aren't a successful swimmer. On the other hand, if you are completing the race in twenty-two seconds, you are a successful swimmer.

In swimming as in all sports, there are always winners and losers. This can be measured with time (the fastest wins) or with a score. It doesn't matter which way it's measured; it is always clear in a very objective way who's successful and who's not.

There are other areas in which the result is somewhat objective but not as much as in sports. If someone works for a company, especially a big multinational company, there is a tool that measures the performance of every employee. Every year, the employee needs to agree with his or her boss what the objectives are going to be for the current year. There are usually around five. At the end of the year, the employee is rated so he or she can clearly know if he or she has done well or not. If the employee has done well, there is a good possibility of getting promoted someday, earning more money, and so on. The goals are not as objective as those in sports, because these tools are not perfect, so many times the goals aren't the right ones, or the importance of each goal isn't fair. Maybe some goals can't be reached because circumstances were out of the employee's hands, among other factors.

The point is that if you are an employee of this type of company, you can know if you're successful or not. But it is not that clear because success in a job is not only how you do in a specific year, but also what your career projections are for the coming years. That part is usually not as clear, and it creates a lot of anxiety for employees because even though they have completed a great year in terms of results, many times that is not directly related to the future. As an employee you don't know if you are, for example, considered a part of the group with high potential; that is usually a secret among a few people in the higher ranks. So if you had a great year but you are not classed as having a high potential, there is a strong possibility that your future will be staying at what you are doing because you know how to do it, but supposedly you don't have the potential for greater responsibility. It's important to notice something here. In this case, the employee can't know exactly if he is successful or not. It's not public data as with a professional athlete, for example.

There is a way that you can have more insight into whether you're successful at a company: this is in relation to how many times you get promoted. Only those with good perspectives, good attributes, good networking, and great achievements get promoted. These promotions always go with more money on the table, and that money is a form of success. The promotions are even more important when someone is selected to be an expat. If someone gets expat status in a corporation, it is a great symbol of success. According to the last 2017 report of expats,[27] there are an estimated 56 to 57 million people living outside their countries. Of those, 11 percent are expats, meaning they were sent by their employers, and this includes those in the diplomatic service. That means that around 6 million people in the world are transferred; that may sound like a lot, but that is only around[28] 0.2 percent[29] of the world's work force.

In summary, talking about office jobs, perhaps not all people are successful, but every employee in some way knows how things are going with their performance and career development.

If a mountain climber reaches Annapurna Summit, the top of the world most dangerous mountain, he or she can feel successful. In that sport summiting one of the fourteen mountains over 8,000 meters and getting down alive is success; it doesn't matter how long it takes.

If someone's a movie star you measure their success with an Oscar. If someone's a painter and his or her paintings are in New York's MOMA's permanent collection, or selling for more than a million dollars, he or she is successful.

Choose any career. It's clear that all of them rate you in a certain way, leaving you with the knowledge of how successful you are.

One of the most important factors related to happiness besides being in a good marriage is your career success. It's a combination of career, health, having someone to love, and money. This is not a rule, but it is a summary with which many people would agree. The interest and challenge of these four attributes is that they are all interconnected. They are like a table designed with four legs. If one is not working, the table is in trouble. It's not enough having three out of four. You need all of them.

Health is another factor in life that is affected by being a parent, due to the lack of time and resources to take care of it.

There is no definitive research into the happiness of couples with and without children. There are pros and cons in both cases. It differs from other studies of married couples regardless of whether they have children or not. In general, married couples are happier than single individuals.

The study, "Parenthood and Happiness: Effects of Work-Family Reconciliation Policies in 22 OECD Countries."[30] analyzes who is happier in each of these countries: those who are parents or those who are not:

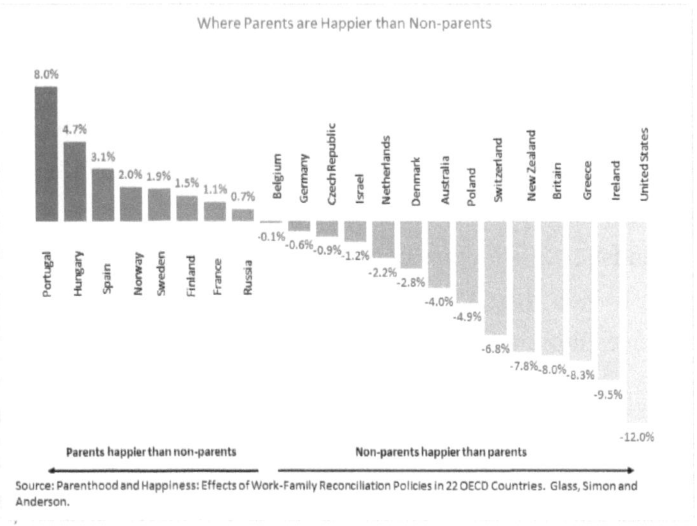

Source: Parenthood and Happiness: Effects of Work-Family Reconciliation Policies in 22 OECD Countries. Glass, Simon and Anderson.

These results are quite surprising in the sense that while it's supposed to be common sense that having kids improves your happiness—parents usually say so and even recommend it to anyone who's in doubt—it looks like parents are kind of envious of those who don't have children, so they want to drag them into the same misery!

Some things might be happening with these shocking results. Most people planning to have kids are not looking for "reviews" of having kids. That's a little absurd. People love to read reviews of everything they plan to consume. One of the things that has driven Amazon to its current success is that it emphasizes reviews. If someone is going on vacation or purchasing a car, a book, or a stapler, almost any purchase, they read reviews.

The reviews are mainly done on purchases that involve three things: a significant amount of money, as with a car; a high risk of failure with bad consequences, as with a carbon monoxide house alarm; and something that must be worth the time you're going to spend on it, as in the case of a book. So dedicating time to checking reviews is undoubtedly important but not as important as "Let's review having kids," a concept affecting most of the population, the greatest expense in their life, and the most demanding of their time.

Statistics tell us that once someone is married, they will begin to gain weight,[31] and once they have their first kid, they gain even more weight.[32] Single people are the ones who keep their weight under control, followed by those who are married without kids.

In terms of being healthier, a few things should be considered: self-commitment, time, and money. Here, as we've seen before, time and money are important. To eat healthier, you should dedicate time to cooking which becomes more difficult when you have kids. If you decide to go out occasionally, you are more likely to end up going to a fast-food chain, which is usually the kid's favorite place. (Nonparents were 73 percent more likely to say they "never" go to a fast-food chain.[33]) If you are conscientious in your workdays and decide to eat healthier, but you don't have time to cook, there is another option: buying prepared healthy food every day. Yes, it does exist; the problem is that you need much more money. That's one of the places where time and money correlate.

Love is very important in life. It's common to hear that if you haven't loved, you haven't lived. It might be true. The book, *Triumphs of Experience*[34] which is based on seventy years of research on a group of people, concludes that happiness is love.

As several studies done over decades conclude, kids make marriage worse, and it is something that affects not only the point touched above about career, but also love itself. Getting married or having a stable partner is the best way to make that love grow or at least stay the same. Adding kids to the equation is going to make love plummet eventually.[35]

Another important reason people decide to have kids is to avoid regretting not doing so in the future. Not for those "now" moments but for future moments, thinking that life will be sadder alone than sharing it with kids. Fortunately for those who are still in doubt about having children and worrying about that lonely future, there is Norwegian research[36] that surveyed people from forty to eighty years old. It concluded, "Women with children have *slightly* more life satisfaction than the ones without children." That wasn't the case for men. More interesting is that "Childless older women and men reported no increased sense of loneliness or depression compared to those who had children." In terms of happiness, people in Western countries are better off without children. In some Eastern European countries and China for example, this is not the case. This is because care services are not as good, and people rely more on their families to help with the problems of aging.

There are two possible options:

The first, as mentioned before, is that they might decide on the easiest route in life to avoid putting pressure on themselves to be successful in something provable. They translate that pressure to the kid, so the kid must prove to the world what the parents couldn't. The parents come to their kids with propositions, such as "I want you to be a top professional tennis player." The question is why wasn't the parent that top professional tennis player. "I want you to get into Princeton," and the kid never asks, "Why didn't you go there?" The parents' usual excuse is "I didn't have the opportunity." Well, everybody has the opportunity to win the Boston Marathon. You just need some good shoes; that great book "Advance Marathoning"[37] which costs around ten dollars; and to wake up every day and run. It's almost free, everybody (with non-disabilities) has that opportunity. The parents want to put the kids under the sort of pressure they didn't put themselves under. They want to see their dreams being realized through another person.

The second is that the concept of parenthood might be debunked. Sadness and loneliness without children are not as many people imagine, it is just a fallacy. Intuition doesn't work trying to get this information right. What does is reading objective studies about it. Maybe people have been making the wrong trade-off in their lives without thinking correctly.

Depending on the country you live in, happiness may be enhanced by being childless. As we saw in the previous chart, 64 percent of the OECD countries selected for the study reported that childless people are happier than people with kids.

Is it smart to leave all your dreams behind while having kids to fulfill your supposed future loneliness and sadness? Or clever not to be responsible for reaching your goals and masking your failure with the perfect excuse that you have given up your life for your kids?

## CHAPTER FIVE

LIVING ABROAD

There are different reasons for living abroad. Some of them involve huge opportunities while other times, it's the only alternative someone has. Having the chance to go as an expat is something few people can enjoy.

Two terms are commonly used for someone in a country other than his or her own. One is *expat*, which has a positive connotation, and the other one is *immigrant*, which is mostly used when someone goes to a new country in not so good financial and/or legal conditions. Both mean that someone is living temporarily or permanently outside their own country. The positive or negative connotation is not something official; it's more how people got used to referring to the condition. Immigrants can be with or without official permission to reside in a specific country. On the other hand, expat is not a term used for someone in another country illegally. It's used exclusively for someone going as part of a multinational company or on his or her own but always in good conditions.

Living in a country other than the one in which you were raised gives you the opportunity to grow in a number of ways. It may improve your professional experience and might allow you to become more profoundly involved with your partner (if you have one) because he or she is the only person you can rely on. Living abroad is also an opportunity to discover new cultures and, meet different kinds of people and in some cases might involve learning a new language. It sounds like everything is positive.

For this analysis let's not consider the economic situation in which people move, which can be positive or negative. Quite often, if the person moves as an employee of a multinational company, their economic situation is going to be better. On the other hand, if someone must go to a new country as a refugee, his or her conditions aren't going to be good, at least in the short term. Let's assume the economic condition is the same in both places so other issues can be considered in the analysis. This is a better way to analyze this situation because a much better economic condition in one place could give it a great advantage over the other. That's why eliminating it is a more objective way to highlight some other differences, whether they be pros or cons.

On the lists of things that most people consider essential to their happiness, besides professional development and economic growth, are good relations with family and friends and proximity and frequent contact with them. These are theoretically the things that make us very happy, and not having them would make our lives just a little above a feeling of misery.

Making friends after college is quite complicated. Most people feel it's a difficult task, and it's even worse when one is in a different country where the culture is not similar or there are language barriers. People make friends in childhood and college years because the conditions for making friends at that stage of life are optimal. The recipe for making friends is quite clear: having interests in common, spending a lot of time together so you can create a shared history, having similar values, and having equal roles.[38] Ideally, that means both should support the other equally. All these conditions are easy to develop at a young age. Constant contact usually starts with unplanned interactions, which in time become planned interactions. In social terms, people are more innocent when young and don't have that many expectations of a new friend. There are not as many things involved in creating rapport with another person as there are with older people. It's easier in the early years when things come more naturally.

Once people complete their college years and start working, there may be a very different kind of person at the office. The group is less homogeneous, and sometimes it isn't homogeneous at all. Indeed, many times it isn't homogeneous on purpose. Each person has a different background and their own interests, and not everyone is at the same stage in their lives, which makes the interaction more difficult. In summary, not everybody feels comfortable meeting new people as potential friends. Most of them are seen as coworkers. Others feel obligated to have a relationship with each other, even though sometimes there isn't any chemistry at all.

Even if you find someone with whom you feel comfortable, spending a lot of time together, ranging from planned to unplanned contact, is not easy. In adult life people have a lot of responsibilities, and dedicating time to a prospective friend is not easy. To complicate matters even more, in the corporate world people move through a lot of positions. Sometimes you have a certain proximity because the job requires contact with one specific person, but when you or the other person gets promoted or transferred to a new position or decides to go to a different company, the natural contact is no longer as frequent. If the link wasn't strong, the relationship easily vanishes.

Apart from the work situation, making new friends in a new city isn't an easy thing. Participating in activities like sports can help with one of the steps to making friends, which is to have some interest in common. Even though this is an opportunity to meet new people, it still remains difficult. It also depends on how open people in a specific culture are to making new friends. There are some countries where people are very reserved, and making friends is extremely difficult—Scandinavian countries, for example. There are others, such as Latin American countries, where it is easier to make friends.

If having friends and extended family is so important to someone's happiness, why does it take second place when he or she decides to emigrate? For people who emigrate for reasons outside their control—as refugee for example—it's clear that this might not be their first or best option. When people decide to emigrate from rich countries, it's usually because they want to, not because they have to. Even though in rich countries, not everybody is able to emigrate, and even though it might be difficult, the numbers aren't negligible. In the case of France, 2.6 percent of the population is living abroad, in Switzerland 7.4 percent, in the United Kingdom 6.8 percent, in Ireland 17.5 percent, in Germany 4.5 percent, in Spain 2 percent, in Italy 4.3 percent, in New Zealand 14.1 percent, in Luxembourg 12.1 percent, and in Iceland 11.7 percent.[39]

We can divide the people who decide to live abroad for positive reasons into three main categories: those moving for retirement, a job opportunity and love.[40]

For those who retired abroad, it's debatable whether it's a choice or a need. Many decide to retire abroad mainly to make their money last longer, they move to a country where the cost of living is much cheaper. There are many rankings detailing the best spots for retirement. These present many different aspects to weight the decision, but the main aspect by far is cost/benefit. While the benefit is somehow subjective those best spots focus more on which cheap place (objective) you can have a decent life in (subjective). If that were not the main driver of the ranking, many of the spots leading the list would be places like Malibu, Palm Beach, Monaco, or Cap Ferrat. People who have enough money when they retire choose whatever and wherever they want. The very rich might even choose to have several houses around the globe and stay in each one for a few months a year. They don't just stick to one specific place. Other rich people don't bother selecting those countries in the rankings of best places for retirement like Costa Rica, Mexico, or Panama. They choose to go to Florida, California, or the south of France, among other fancy places.

The main reasons people decide to live abroad for retirement are:[41]

- Financial reasons: If they don't have much money and want to stretch their money as far as possible, they can choose to live in a cheaper country. On the other hand, if they have a lot of money, they can choose a location that in their opinion is better than their native country.
- Quality of life: Warmer weather is high on the list of priorities, along with a high quality of life, in the sense that they can afford more things because of the lower cost of living in the host country.

For the ones who decide to live in another country for work:

- Economic incentives: It can be a good job offer, a transfer to a different country, or tax incentives. In the case of a job offer, the host country usually offers more opportunities than their home country. It could be due to a temporary economic decline or lack of opportunities at home for a specific career.
- New experiences: The current situation in their country is not bad, but they want to experience new things in life. They also have a dream country to live in.
- Adventure: They don't like where they're living, and as an adventure, they go somewhere else to give themselves a second chance to enjoy life.

Going abroad for reasons of love:

- Falling in love: Someone falls in love with someone else and decides to go one step further and emigrate so they can be together.
- Going as a couple: Someone has a job offer in a different country, and his or her partner decides to go along, basically for love.

Why are there around 57 million expats legally abroad in the world[42] when the most important thing for happiness is having close friends and family and these people appear to be lacking this? Are they sacrificing happiness for something else? Maybe they have friends and family, but the supposed key ingredient for that happiness is to have close contact with them, and obviously these expats are not having this either.

Let's see how satisfied expats in several countries are.[43]

Percentage of people satisfied with living abroad:
- Americans   84%
- French   84%
- Swiss   82%
- British   81%
- Irish   80%
- Germans   79%
- Spanish   78%
- Italians   78%

Is it really the case that extended family and friends are more important than other things in life? It's been proved that, for example, a single person or a couple without kids can be very happy. An adult man or woman can be happy once their parents have gone. Even parents who have lost their kids can be happy after a few years of recovery. An only child can be totally normal, happy, and comfortable without siblings. People who divorce can be perfectly happy again after a while. Therefore, for people in general, good relationship can make their lives more joyful, but it seems that it isn't indispensable for happiness as some people insist.

If people are so dependent on family and friends, why are so many expats reporting a high level of life satisfaction without having close or daily contact with family and friends? The list above is from people of developed countries where, in most cases, people choose to go to live. They are voluntarily choosing not to be with their friends and families and they are totally comfortable with it. If you are thinking that maybe they go abroad temporarily to make money or to have an adventure or experience, that is not necessarily the case, since 29 percent said that they might be living abroad forever. For example, in the case of people going abroad to Canada, 45 percent consider staying there forever, and of the ones going to France, 40 percent want to remain there for the rest of their lives.

Another thing to consider is marriage or union between people of different nationalities. If the premise of the importance of family and friends in someone's happiness is true, why do so many people marry those of different nationalities whom they got to know while living in a different country temporarily? In these cases, one or both are sacrificing their friends and family from their country for life. It's logical to assume that they are doing it voluntarily, so there must be several other things that are more important to making such a decision.

It seems that people who haven't chosen the option of having an experience abroad hide themselves by saying, the most important thing in life is family and friends. The perfect investigation would be to make a job offer in an amazing city to all those people, who said they wouldn't go because of the family and friends, until is attractive enough to accept it. Then wait for a while to make that study again to see if they have changed their mind about living abroad. So, "Hey José, you were saying living in Managua with your friends and family is best because you have the most important things in life. You must have been miserable these last two years in Vancouver, weren't you?" Or even better: "Hey Franco, you must be missing the salary you used to earn while you were living in Buenos Aires. Argentine pesos devaluated from four to one in 2012 to forty to one in September 2018 versus the US dollar. Poor guy, now earning in euros. You must be very sad missing your friends back home! How do you live with that?"

The people giving their opinion of how good their lives are in those rich countries mentioned above are not necessarily rich and don't have all the choices in life. One way to be objective is to look at how people who have the means to live however they want are living. Let's see if how they are living reflects that the most important element of enjoying life is being close to their extended family and those longtime friends.

There is a group of people in the world who we couldn't say are happy or the happiest group or have the highest values or are some kind of Greek philosophers who know exactly how they should live to optimize happiness. They are maybe the opposite, and who knows if they are making the best decisions on how to handle life. What we can say about them is that they are famous, powerful, smart and rich; have special abilities; and have something few people in this world have: the power to choose. Let's see:

- Of the top one hundred *Fortune* 500 CEOs. 90 percent of them don't live in their hometowns.[44] (See Appendix A).
- Of the top twenty highest-paid actors,[45] 95 percent of them don't live in their hometowns. (See Appendix B).
- Of the top twenty-five highest-paid musicians[46] (excluding groups), 84 percent of them don't live in their hometowns. (See Appendix C).
- Of the top thirty-five tennis players in the ATP ranking,[47] 74 percent of them don't live in their hometowns. Curiously, 23 percent of them live in Monaco. (See Appendix D).
- Of the twenty current Formula 1 drivers,[48] 80 percent don't live in their hometowns. Even more

> extreme than the tennis players, 47 percent of them live in Monaco. (See Appendix E).
>
> - Of the top thirty golfers in the Professional Golfers' Association (PGA) ranking,[49] 97 percent of them don't live in their hometowns. (See Appendix F).

It might seem that sports professionals, are living temporarily in new locations because it gives them an edge for their profession. It might be that in the selected city there are better coaches, better fields, better weather or better life that they can afford. It's quite difficult to be a professional golfer in Montreal where you have temperatures of -22 degrees Fahrenheit in winter. It's a must for those in many professions to live in a place where they have access to things key to their success. The average career of a professional tennis player ranked in the top ten is 16.0 years for men and 15.8 years women.[50] If it's a sacrifice being in a city other than their own for that profession, it is quite a long period of sacrifice. It is not usually said that the most important thing in life is your profession.

An interesting thing to consider is what happens when these tennis players retire? (See Appendix G). Well, 73 percent of the top players still decide to live away from their hometowns once they have retired.[51] Basically, it is the same percentage of the current top players in the ranking living away from their hometowns. Why do so many choose Monaco? It's clear that the main driver of rich people living in Monaco is tax purposes; other reasons are that it is a very safe place, and it's a country where paparazzi are not welcomed, so they can have a private life and make their living without being stalked.

A clear majority of professional golfers are American (49 percent of the PGA top 100 ranking).[52] They can't live in

Monaco for tax purposes because Americans pay taxes on their worldwide income. So it's assumed that Monaco is not an attractive place for them. So what is the Monaco of American professional golfers? Florida, where there's no state income tax. Where in Florida is the best place to live as a professional golfer? Jupiter.

Do these professional golfers prefer to pay low taxes or be with family and friends? Definitely, they choose low taxes, so we can deduce that makes them happier. Wait a minute… how about if most of them are there not because of low taxes but because of the year-round nice weather to play golf, great golf courses, and community of other professional golfers? Not really—67 percent of top golfers still prefer to live somewhere other than their hometowns once retired.[53] So no, they don't prefer to be with their families and longtime friends. (See Appendix H).

In real life, few people know or care what studies say about what makes them happier. Instinctively, they know that having a family and some friends usually makes their life better. It is something almost everybody can have. Friends and family come in life as a default (with certain exceptions). To make the decision whether they prefer being with friends and family to other experiences, people don't go to statistics; they go to trial and error. That's the way they recognize what is better for their lives, which turns out to be a personal decision. The problem is that for most of the population, the luxury of trial and error is almost impossible; 99 percent can't live in a penthouse in Monaco for a few years to know if that gives them happiness so later they can decide whether to stick with it or ditch it. Considering something less fancy, it's almost impossible for most people just to live in a different country or in their dream city. The visa requirements, finding a job abroad et cetera, turn out to be extremely difficult if not impossible for most. As most people can't make that trial and error and don't have the determination to analyze, investigate, or search for options, they just stay in what they instinctively and perhaps wrongly say is better for them. The ones who are fortunate enough to be in a position where they can use trial and error or decide to see options, are objectively choosing something different than what their gut feelings are telling them but what makes their lives more fulfilled. They don't care about their intuition, what they care about is what their lives, thinking in an objective and logical way, are giving them.

With a lot of money, you can't buy friends or extended family, but you can buy a residence permit or a citizenship. If you are one of those who think that happiness is something away from your hometown, there are good offers. Nobody assures you a job in these places, but if you can pay (invest) the required amount for that residence, you probably don't need to search for a job. For example, to increase your chances of having a good time, let's take the United Kingdom, which is in the top 20 on the happiness index.[54] Why not live in fancy London? You can have a residence by applying for the Tier 1 Investor Visa.[55] It's easy; just follow these three steps: first you must be present in the United Kingdom; second, pay a fee of £14,966 for you and your wife or husband (if you want a special service with a twenty-four-hour response); and third, invest at least £2,000,000 in government bonds or in actively trading UK-registered companies. As easy as that. If you don't have those pounds, well, better stay happy with your friends and family in your hometown.

Intuition and common knowledge have taught us that happiness mainly comes from having good family ties and good friendships. We intuitively think that conserving these ties while having frequent contact during our lifetime will keep us happy. There is some evidence, as shown in this chapter, that from two different perspectives, people in optimal conditions and with vast opportunities are not choosing this option. It doesn't matter if they are expats coming from rich countries, famous celebrities, or top executives; most of them are not selecting that path. In terms of expats, many of them are so happy living abroad that they are considering staying there forever. On the other hand, the rich and famous, are choosing careers and places they consider better to live in over relations with friends and family. As with the other expats, in most cases they don't get back to their hometowns even after retirement. Why are the decisions of this last group important? Because, they are lucky enough to be in a position that few people attain: they can choose.

## CHAPTER SIX

LIFE CONFIDENTIALITY

Many times we have heard from those who are about to die about what they regret. They have often said, "Live the life that you want, not a life dictated by others."

What does that really mean, and how do we follow that recommendation?

One of the most difficult things in life is knowing how to live it well and what really makes us happy. Is happiness the road, the goal, or both? Or maybe neither? There isn't always a definitive answer.

Let's picture one very common type of person, someone whose day-to-day life consists of work, home, hanging out with friends, and being addicted to social media and WhatsApp.

Sadly, most humans have something I call an internal scorecard (ISC). How well or poorly you score is the result of comparing yourself with others. For example, if you aren't a professional tennis player and you want to have a rating in your ISC, you wouldn't compare your abilities with Roger Federer's. Rather, you would compare yourself with the tennis players at the club where you play. To narrow the comparison more, you would only compare yourself with the ones in your own tennis ladder. If you're in the third level at the club, those are the players you would compare yourself with.

As this example shows, you can get an idea of how everybody compares with you. If you wanted to know how successful your career has been so far, you would compare your net worth to the perceived net worth of people like you—friends, classmates, office peers, neighbors. You would never compare yourself to the ones on the *Forbes* list. If you did, your ISC would be all in red. Along the same lines, you wouldn't compare yourself to the less fortunate people at the bottom of the pyramid in Africa either.

What happens when you compare yourself to others? Comparing is more than thinking "I'm better or worse than someone else." When you make comparisons like this, you're doing more than rating yourself against the other person. These comparisons are all the attitudes you put in your life to make others think that your ISC is better than it really is. Doing this, you fill your life with ideas, expenses, and desires that you really don't want or need.

Here is how to create a good ISC. Well, you can choose not to have an ISC at all, but because that's almost impossible for most people, it's better to have one based only on a comparison with yourself. But how do you do this? The key here is confidentiality.

The less you know about others and the less they know about you, the better your ISC. Here is why. Of course, this is assuming that life's purpose is increasing happiness as a road and as a goal; as was pointed out before, this is not necessarily true, but if you believe it is the case:

Many people travel, spend money, use time, and learn just to project to others an image of who they are. Let's look at some examples:

They like to spend time on exotic vacations just to come back and say, "I went to Southeast Asia," even if being there didn't fulfill their passions. They know that even before going, but taking such a trip shows that they are original, adventurous, and self-confident. Thus, they end up with $6,000 less in their bank account, use up twenty-one days of vacation, and have an experience they won't remember for very long. Worst of all, they might not even enjoy many of the moments of those twenty-one days they were in Thailand or Malaysia.

What if you win a prize: a trip to any place you want, fifteen days for free, including tickets and hotel? The only restriction is that afterwards, you can't tell anyone about it, ever. Would you choose that trip to Antarctica? Or searching for gorillas in Uganda? Some people might; many would not.

Many of the things people do are actually undertaken just to tell people they know that they have done something. These bad decisions always end up with the same outcomes: less money in your account, time wasted, and unfulfilled moments.

A second example is that some people will go to a Rolling Stones concert because a lot of people are going. The cheapest tickets run out in minutes, and the only available ones are no less than $300. Why is everyone going? Some people think, "I don't like the Stones that much, but it might be my last opportunity to see them, and all my friends are going." So they plan to spend $600 for two tickets, just because everyone is going and it might be the last chance to see the Stones... even though they don't like them that much! They don't even consider that it might be a little unpleasant to listen to "Start

Me Up" at 125 decibels. (Anything more than 85 decibels is harmful to your ears.)

Investment in education is another example. In Latin America, most middle-class people send their kids to private schools. There are different price ranges, but the best options can cost around $10,000 a year. These top-tier schools are filled with two types of people: those who can pay for it, and those who can't. So why is it that so many people do it?

Many of them justify their decision with the concept that education is the most important thing you can invest money in. OK, that might be reasonable, but I will say that an important phrase is missing from that sentence. It should be, "…is the most important thing you can invest in with money *that you have*." Here are two types of people: the ones who aren't great with financial planning, and the ones who want to impress others by sending their kids to premium schools. Making this bad decision may get them in serious trouble in their retirement.

Some people like reading for pleasure, others for knowledge, and a third group like to read just to comment about a best-selling book. An average book might take around six hours to read. Investing that amount of energy just to comment about it on your next coffee break with friends won't be a good investment of time and effort. Many people who don't read frequently ask a reader, "What do you recommend?" Maybe the best answer is, "What topic do you like?" Many times reading some friend's favorite book ends up being an extremely boring activity. (That also happens with some Oscar-winning movies that do not necessarily fit everybody's tastes.)

In terms of books, keep in mind that worldwide, there are around two million new titles every year. That means you should be wise when choosing. How wise is reading some popular books just to comment about them at your next coffee klatch?

All these examples go to the same point: spend most of your time on activities that make you happy. How happy can you be if you are spending time, effort, and money on things that apparently improve the perception others have of you?

Life is shorter than you think it is. It passes like a movie. Doing something because it's supposed to be a cool thing; because everybody is doing it; because it is something that every man or woman should do; because if you don't do it you are not a good friend, a good grandchild, or a gentleman.

People should mostly do things that fulfill them. (Not considering must-do things in life as taking out the trash.) They don't come into this world just to please others or to do what's supposed to be the obvious choice or to behave in a certain way in every situation. It's as if one day someone wrote down how one should behave in every single situation in life, and we all must follow that. If someone invites you to their home, you should go and bring a present. If someone dies, you should go to the funeral. You should take your kids to Disney World; you can't miss the soccer World Cup finals or the Super Bowl on TV; and if you are a woman, you should read *Fifty Shades of Grey*. All these *shoulds* people do in life increase anxiety, make them competitive, and cause them to compare themselves to others. We really don't know who created these overrated social rules. It's not important who established them; the important thing is, why is everyone following them?

There are occasions when you can't get out of following these social rules, but the important point is to treat these as exceptions, not as the common behavior. Your main priority should be to try to accomplish what you really like most of the time. This concept should always be in everyone's mind, for every decision they make.

There is an important distinction that can cause confusion: the fact that you don't come into this world to please other people doesn't mean that you shouldn't care about others in order to make a better world. If someone is a manager in a company, it's indisputable that they should care for the people who work there, the stakeholders, and society. If you can help someone who really needs it, that's OK and different from trying to follow some social rules that only make your life more miserable. Those social rules are the ones that push people to live in a way they don't want to. Those "rules" are the ones that make people lose focus in their lives. Avoiding those rules leaves people more time to accomplish what they really care about.

Once you begin questioning every single "you should" rule, you can:

First, think about whether you are with the right life partner. There are some problems in a relationship that can't be solved. Think deeply and, if you aren't with the right person, why don't you search for new options? You can live alone, with a new partner, with a roommate, or in any way you want. If someone fails in a relationship, it is not a reason to be punished for the rest of his or her life. Find a way that is what you really want, not one that follows a rule.

A second step is the kind of meetings you decide to attend. Usually in a corporate environment, you are more obligated to go to a lot of meetings—that is, up to the moment you learn how to say no and prioritize what is important. To reach your professional goals, you need to focus on and attend to what provides value, not to what is merely filling your agenda.

In terms of personal life, the issues are totally different. In your personal life, you aren't paid to attend meetings as is the case in your job. In your personal life, making choices is up to you. You can decide to attend just a few meetings or none at all, only going to the ones that give you full enjoyment.

What is full enjoyment? It's not about laughing every moment, riding a roller coaster, or discovering a cure for cancer. What it is is just what *joy* means. It's not an adrenaline rush or to be confused with simple excitement. It is about being in a moment when you feel glad about yourself. It's about being at peace. It's about not needing anything more than what you've got at that moment. It could also be about being with someone or a group of people, not necessarily being alone. It depends on what each person really likes.

It's very well known that to learn new things, to be good at something, you must get out of your comfort zone. Yes, that is a valid statement. Many might think that having joy is being in your comfort zone, but that has nothing to do with it. Being in a joyful state is highly possible once you get out of your comfort zone, rather than having that regular life filling your time with obligations. Joy can also be challenging to your comfort zone. Doing what others want you to do in your life isn't usually an activity that challenges your comfort zone. It is just an activity commonly accepted by society that delays your growth in any aspect while also not providing any joy.

To clarify this theory, let's look at some examples:

- Going to a funeral: In most cases it is not necessary. It gives you nothing in life besides wasting three hours while being in a depressing atmosphere. You're not going to win or lose a friend because of not attending a funeral. Just make a phone call, have a nice conversation, and make an excuse for not going if it's someone close to you. If it's someone not that close, maybe the phone call isn't even necessary. In the phone call the nice part of it is important; it is not just to say, "Sorry for your loss," because if that's the case, it will be awkward. In other words, it's not taking you out of your comfort zone because it is not challenging you to grow in any respect.

- If you like writing: It is one thing to just write; it's another to be a good writer and have a lot of useful ideas, be very entertaining, or present extensive knowledge of a specific topic. No matter why you want to write, it's definitely challenging, and it'll take you out of your comfort zone. In fact, it takes you out and also provides joy.

There might be many ways to help you decide to do only what you want or like, but one way that's very effective is with confidentiality. You can practice until you become expert in this approach to making decisions. The only thing you must do is have extreme confidentiality in your personal life. If you aren't constantly telling others how and on what you spend your time and money, you won't be making bad decisions. This doesn't mean you must be in complete silence in a meeting. The best way is to put forward topics that people avoid talking about: what they have, do, or spend on. Just general topics. Not general as in superficial—they can be superficial or deep— but general, nothing personal. They can be personal in terms of ideas, but not in terms of things. This goes a little further than saying "Interesting people talk about ideas; others talk about things and people." This is talking about the why of things, searching for options, theories, points of view, not about who has what or who has done what. Better to go with the ideas but without involving personal experiences. If someone is talking about the Louvre's architecture, it's not necessary to say, "Last summer in Paris, I was contemplating the amazing architecture of the Louvre." Avoiding the "last summer" part of the story is preferable. You can learn about the Louvre in other ways that just not just by being there; you can learn about it from a book, a History Channel documentary, and so on. By avoiding the "I was there," you are keeping confidentiality while still participating in an interesting conversation.

It may sound easy and useless, but it isn't. You are changing the way your mind works. Once you gain control over this way of thinking, every decision you make is made because you want to, and you are very confident that it's the best for you. Avoiding the topics of what you have, what you do, and what you want will keep you in line with the strategy. Once you master that, it is highly probable that you will never regret your decisions. If you have doubts about making a decision and you need advice, go to the experts, not to your friends or people you know. It is almost always better to be informed by experts in any field, by blogs, or by big databases where you see average ratings. It is a bad idea to tell a friend, "I have an extra $250,000, and I'm not sure where to invest it." In that case go to a certified financial advisor, read *The Intelligent Investor*[56], or take a course in finance.

If you plan to go to a very fancy hotel, it might be better to see a TripAdvisor rating, where you can see the average of a thousand voters, rather than just asking one friend's opinion. It's worthless to ask only one person. It's much more reliable to take the average of many users. Asking a friend about a fancy hotel may take you on one of two routes:

1. "Hey, I'm planning to go to the Plaza in New York; have you been there? I want to know how good it is." If you go this way, your arrogance is out of this world. It doesn't sound good, and you gain nothing—just someone who would prefer to avoid you.

2. If that friend recommends to you "Yes, go to the Plaza; it's amazing," the story doesn't end there. You might feel pressured to go there because the conversation will continue in the future. Maybe you would like to impress him later by saying that you didn't just go to the Plaza but your flight was also in business class, and you did some shopping at Saks.

Regarding these two outcomes: Do you gain anything? Numbers 1 and 2 aren't better than checking the Plaza reviews on TripAdvisor, so you'd better stick with that.

How about if you decide to purchase some décor for your home? People tend to overspend on housing, whether buying or renting—mostly when buying.[57] The point is how your tastes and housing needs change if you are trying to please others instead of satisfying yourself. If you use the confidentiality strategy, nobody is going to know how you live, so all your decisions in terms of space or décor will be just for you. As a result, you'll end up buying what you really like. That doesn't mean you're going to live in an ugly place because you're not inviting anyone to or telling anyone about your home. You can go eccentric if you really want and buy sterling silver flatware. Just go for it, but you won't need to buy the eight-person set; just go for the two-person set (or the size of your family).

Many people say, "I love having friends at home." That may be true, but it's a little sacrifice to reach your goal and improve that ISC. That doesn't mean you should stop seeing your friends. It's just better doing it at a neutral place, where ideas are involved, not things.

All that overspending just to please others will be highly regrettable in the future. Remember all the times you went to a fancy restaurant with a big group of friends just because someone organized it, and you went without analyzing it and ended up being nothing special. Something you don't really enjoy.

In terms of "universe time," our lives are just a simple spot on the canvas. If we want to live life to the fullest in such a short time, it's better to optimize time, spending it on what we really like. Comparing ourselves to others causes us to make very bad decisions. Being confidential about our lives helps us automatically select what is best for us—optimizing time on what we love to do and spending money wisely.

## CHAPTER SEVEN

SCAN FOR IMPORTANT INFORMATION

In college, in the news, and in general conversations, we always hear about the lives of extraordinary people. Those are the people we should compare ourselves to, in a sense that we should take lessons out of their lives so we can apply some of them to our reality. This way, someday we might be as successful as they are.

That is one of the reasons that many people read biographies of important men or women. They write their stories because they are very successful, and that's why people buy them. Among the nonfiction books in existence, biographies are the ones closest to fiction. Not in the sense that they are not true, but in the sense that they make you dream in such an unreal way. They are as impossible as a novel that presents that type of life or invites you to accomplish something similar.

Take for instance the biographies of Steve Jobs, Phil Knight, and Richard Branson. They are all incredible books about incredible characters, very entertaining and very useful in terms of understanding a little deeper how they think, how their businesses work, and how they made billions. The problem with these books is that they don't teach you anything that you can apply in your real life. It can even be dangerous because you might try to copy some lifestyles, which usually involve characters with extremely low-risk aversion, and you might quit your job to develop your incredible idea, ending up with nothing more than debts, time lost in your career, and burnout.

All these biographies are of outliers, who by definition are very rare, the exceptions in the world. By 2015, the number of billionaires in the world was around two thousand.[58] From those two thousand around one thousand were self-made billionaires. So, the percentage of the world's 7 billion people who are billionaires is 0.00000014. In a supposed scenario where everybody in the world is planning to develop a new idea and become a billionaire, what is the probability of entering that select group?

So rather than reading all these books, apart from the fact that they are very entertaining and inspiring, it's important to read information that can be useful to improving your life with a much higher probability of success than all those zeros in the billionaire probability percentage.

Many people dream about the goal, not about the process. Many want easy money, not hard-earned money. Many want to work minimal hours and earn millions. Most of these billionaires didn't have an easy road; that's why they write about it in the first place. If it had been very easy, it wouldn't be that interesting writing about it. All these stories are usually about self-made billionaires. It's really outstanding to be worth billions when you started with almost nothing. It wouldn't be as interesting reading the trials of someone who inherited their fortune, unless they did something amazing besides inheriting.

If someone wins $100 million in the lottery, he or she is probably not going to write a book about it. There is no process here; it involved just buying the ticket. That's why the process is the important part of all these stories. What if you were to read about a process that catapults you not exactly to being a billionaire but to something that gives you the opportunity to have a very comfortable life, doing what you want to do?

This process is having a strategy that should work every day. That's the opposite of easy money. It's earning good money, the result of work done over a lot of years and with a lot of sacrifices. With it you will end up with something like the same feeling these billionaires have. Billionaires are not necessarily happy. Those who consider themselves happy are not happy because of the money. As Google founder Sergey Brin once said, "You always hear the phrase, money doesn't buy you happiness. But I always in the back of my mind figured a lot of money will buy you a little bit of happiness. But it's not really true."[59]

With this in mind, it doesn't matter if you earn one or two million or billions. After acquiring enough money that you have all the basics covered and more, your happiness stops growing. So I'm convinced of the worth of the expression "Think big", or as a professor of mine once said: "You need investors, but ask them not for a hundred thousand dollars; you should ask for a million dollars." That is thinking big. Usually the small businesses are the ones that close their doors in the first five years.[60] Perhaps with big business, the probability of succeeding is higher; I'm not sure about that. Others say, "Aim high, and you will hit a higher level than if you aim at something that is too conservative."

It is obviously better to have billions than millions; if we're speaking about money, more is always better. The problem here is the probability of reaching one or the other. In the case of trying to make billions, you might end up with nothing. Your intuition wouldn't be much help in taking you there. In contrast, the one or two billion strategies that will never get you billions but will allow you to achieve the million mark are much more probable. It's something akin to selecting a career: for example, being a tennis player or being a lawyer. If you regularly rank in the top fifty in the Association of Tennis Professionals (ATP), you will be making millions. If you are a lawyer and you are smart about your money, you can easily end up with one million. If you don't succeed as a tennis player, you won't have money for your basics, and that's a serious issue. As a lawyer if things aren't going that great, well, you can still have life savings of around that million mark.

It may sound like common sense to copy what successful people have done. It seems that they have done it following some of their own rules. The problem is that all those successful people had unique abilities in some unique conditions; that makes their success difficult to duplicate. The most rational thing to do if you want success is to follow a path with a high rate of achievement.

Are we all too obsessed with the lives of those famous characters, and are we constantly minimizing the more simplistic but effective ideas?

## CHAPTER EIGHT

OVERRATING UNHEALTHY FOOD

One of the main ways people enjoy life is through eating. It is the main activity when someone plans to do something for leisure. Every plan is usually based around food. Besides going to a restaurant, which is directly an eating plan, examples include going to someone's house to chat, going to a basketball game, and going out to a bar; all of them involve food. Some people even end their gym sessions with a protein shake or a smoothie. This is not just in a specific city, country, or culture. It's everywhere. Food is the central part of most plans.

This idea of liking unhealthy food came from our parents and from the society in which we were raised. It's just the way we grew up, indulging in flavors that supposedly are delicious for us. During our first years of life, maybe from ages zero to five, there is quite an interest among parents in giving their children a lot of healthy products. After that, somehow parents aren't as strict as in those first years of life, and selecting types of food becomes more flexible. The thinking has become that anything you eat is OK, as long as you eat something.

Kids grow up eating whatever they want, usually eating a lots of junk food into their teen years due to their lack of money and addiction to those types of flavors. They reach a certain age when they are more mature and start realizing that the food they've been eating for almost all their lives is not good for them, but they really love the flavor—a flavor that seems impossible to stop loving. Those branded products are already part of them; they're part of our culture and part of us. Those are brands we totally identify with. Not just the flavor but the amazing way of life that those brands have tried to brainwash us into adopting over the years. Sadly, in many cases, they have reached their goal.

Taking this into consideration, there is a general feeling that only food that is considered bad for our health is delicious and makes us happy. If someone is eating a broccoli plate with a smile on his face, people feel sorry for him. "Poor guy, he doesn't know the pleasures of life."

The dolce vita concept of living your life to its fullest with great pleasures is how some people define the purpose of their lives. Why have an apple when you can enjoy half a jar of Nutella?

Why is there so much self-indulgence in life when it comes to food?

One important reason people get attached to unhealthy food is because they overestimate how easy it is to adapt to a healthy diet. Let's compare food with several other aspects of life to see how it's different:

If you are one of those who love la dolce vita, or at least understand the concept, here are several items to analyze. Many luxury items are made only for a few to enjoy. Think about a Bugatti, a car worth $3 million that's in the realm of extreme exclusivity. If you talked with a car lover, he or she would tell you that it's an amazing car, generally speaking. Even he or she had a Ford Mustang and was really happy with it, under no circumstances would he or she say that the Ford is better than the Bugatti. It may make better cost/benefit sense to have the Ford, but in terms of the car itself, without considering the cost, there is nothing to argue. The highest probability is that he or she never thinks about not having a Bugatti or is somehow sad because of his or her misfortune in not having the money to purchase that car. In summary, he or she knows there are better things that what he or she has got, but he or she is OK and happy with it.

How about crossing the Atlantic Ocean in business class? There are only a few people who pay for business-class tickets on their own. Usually people travel in that class because the company they work for pays for the ticket, or they get an upgrade. The vast majority of travelers fly coach. As with the previous car example, it's agreed traveling business class is better than traveling coach, not considering the price. But does that mean that the coach traveler is unhappy sitting there for around ten hours while crossing the Atlantic? Not much. Mainly they are happy because they are on vacation. Maybe those are not the most comfortable ten hours of their lives, but all the same, their happiness might be very high on the scale. They don't need to travel in business class to be happy, and it doesn't make a significant difference on their happiness scale. It might be that people at least once in their lifetimes have the chance to fly in business class on a transatlantic flight and might remember and miss that type of experience. The ones who never had that experience will not even think about it. The point here is that people are usually happy traveling coach even though business class is better.

What's the difference with food? As with many other items, preferences are totally objective in terms of tastes. A Bugatti is better than a Ford, Brioni is better than the Gap, and Palm Beach is better than San Pedro Sula. Nobody discusses that.

Food in terms of nutrients is the same as the examples above somehow. Nobody debates if a doughnut is healthier than an apple, Oreo is better than broccoli or Häagen-Dazs is better than plain oatmeal. Now how about the taste?

A kid might say that Froot Loops is his or her favorite food. It is not likely that an adult would say that.

Americans in general are addicted to junk food. Many consider that type of food their favorite even though they clearly know it's not the healthiest choice. They are choosing it for its flavor, then for the cost, and do not even consider how healthy it is. According to research in neurobiology of food addiction, people are neurochemically driven to choose junk food because the brain feels something similar to a drug addiction.[61] This type of addiction is not an incurable disease. Many people stop eating junk food and change to the right options for a healthy lifestyle.

The point is that matters of taste are very subjective when it comes to food. There are foods that create addiction, so the body craves that type of food. Foods with high fat and refined sugar content are very addictive. Take for example a doughnut. Technically, what happens when you eat foods like this is that the brain releases higher amounts of dopamine (one of the neurotransmitters that make us happy). The body, to regulate this higher-than-normal amount, starts removing dopamine receptors to keep the body in balance. The fewer dopamine receptors the brain has, the more of the food the person needs to be rewarded with the same amount of dopamine. The more the person eats, the fatter and unhealthier he or she gets.

Here comes the concept of acquired tastes. People get used to some flavors; the more they eat them, the more they like them. Do you think anyone ever enjoyed their very first sip of beer? A kid trying anchovies or olives? A teenager trying his or her first cognac?

These are examples of acquired tastes. At first, they taste terrible, but in time people end up liking them.

Here comes the tricky part. When someone starts eating the "correct" food—meaning legumes, whole grains, vegetables, fruits and nuts—their tastes start to change. Their body and mind start to forget about those chocolate chip cookies they used to crave, each time wanting more. The tricky part is that their tastes change, and what they used to love, they don't love anymore. It is not like the Bugatti that the car fanatic will always like even though they can't have it. In this case, they can choose the chocolate chip cookie if they want; the thing is that they don't want it anymore. What was an amazing flavor for the common population turns out to be a simple sugary taste that seems unnatural to their body. In this sense, eating healthy food turns out to be no sacrifice at all. It is like having the Bugatti for the Mustang price! The best of both worlds.

The important thing to remember is that it takes time for this to happen. Time is important because you need to get used to this new type of flavor. Flavors are not good or bad in an intrinsic sense. Flavors are good in terms of what we are used to eating. Most of the food we like is what we learned to eat since we were kids. In the United States it might be a hamburger; in China it might be a scorpion; and in the Amazon jungle, monkey brains.

Time is important so people get used to the flavor and to the effect that this food produces in their bodies. One common effect of becoming vegetarian is feeling weak and dizzy. Sometimes it's because vegetarians eat less food than those on an omnivore diet. They don't realize that, although they may be eating the same volume of food, vegetarian food has far fewer calories than animal-based food. Later, people start to balance portions to figure out the amount they should eat. That's only one of the symptoms; another is the body getting used to plant instead of animal nutrients. The best of all the consequences is starting to lose a lot of weight.

The world has an obesity epidemic. Among the many reasons, one that is very important and that few consider, is that people overrate flavor and underrate adaptation to new tastes. They allow their intuition to choose which food is more delicious because it makes them happier. The usual reason is "Because I love cookies," or "I love hamburgers." That love is totally changeable. There are things you used to like as a child that you don't necessarily like them anymore and vice versa. As a teenager you are in a growing period, so you need more food than an adult. That is temporary. Some teenagers get used to junk food because of convenience and price, but when they switch to healthy food, their preferences change. What used to taste delicious doesn't taste that way anymore. Their taste evolves; it isn't something permanent.

People usually say, "I can't stop eating KFC because it's delicious." The good news is that love is not forever; it is provisional until you get used to new flavors. Something strange happens. Not only do you not crave those tastes you used to love anymore, but you also feel some level of revulsion, and when you eat them, sometimes you can't digest them as well as before. For example, for vegans, many times the smell of animal food turns disgusting, and sweets turn out to be too sweet.

To make that change to healthy food and feel it naturally inside you, you shouldn't accept the common belief that it takes a minimum of twenty-one days to create a habit, which is not science based. In reality, a study determined that it takes from two to eight months, with an average of sixty-six days, to make something into a habit.[62] In yoga and meditation courses, teachers usually recommend the twenty-one-day technique, which is originally taken from the book Psycho-Cybernetics,[63] but that isn't fact based.

A curious thing is that many people make some effort in different aspects of life but not when it comes to food. To learn anything in life, you need time (among a lot of other things), obviously. Talent, dedication, emotion, focus, and passion are also needed. For some things you need money, contacts, teachers, mentors, coaches, et cetera. But the focus on time here is because learning anything important in life takes time. People accept, for example, that to learn to speak French, you need around a year. To learn to play the violin, no less than five years. What makes these two examples different from eating healthy? One might think that the difference with learning French or the violin is the motivation. In these cases, people who decide to learn are motivated for sure. It doesn't make much sense to dedicate a year or five years to something you don't like.

In the case of food, people are not motivated to change. They think that every type of food out there it's OK as long as you consume it in moderation. They don't want to lose what they already have: the delicious flavor of steak or brownies. The motivation is very low to decide to drop that. The taste of those foods is much stronger than some purported results from changing eating habits. They also think that if they lose that precious flavor, their life is not going to be the same. They think they are changing their personality, something that is part of them, but that's definitely not the case.

It's important to realize that after you align your life with healthy habits, reaching the goal is more fulfilling than the small sacrifice suffered for some few days or months. That initial sacrifice will not last long, but the fulfillment of having to interiorize something new in your life might last forever. It's like the pain of studying for four months to take the GRE in contrast to the joy of having a master's degree.

If people realize this, there will be far fewer deaths due to cardiac arrest, cancer, diabetes, and several other ailments. It's just waiting for the right time until your tastes evolve toward something healthy.

Eating whatever we want because we can control what we eat and what we don't in a natural way doesn't work. Intuitively eating what our mothers used to cook for us when we were kids doesn't work either as the best diet for our health. If you think that a registered dietitian (RD) doesn't have any more knowledge than the general population about how we should eat, think again. That RD should have some additional knowledge after studying for five years. So why do people trust their poor knowledge on what to put in their mouths? Why do they lose the battle with flavor addiction, ignoring the principles of how tastes evolve, instead of sticking to a good diet? Better not go with your intuition on this. There's a lot of information out there to be used, and better, trust the professional.

## CHAPTER NINE

UNDERESTIMATING PERIODIC SMALL EXPENSES

"Watch the pennies, and the dollars will take care of themselves,"[64] is an aphorism to have in mind while reading this chapter.

Spending money is the least of the things you can use your gut feelings on. When using numbers, you use pure logic. It's worth nothing imagining that something is less expensive through time than it really is.

Let's start with these charts taken from the 2017 Global Wealth Report.[65]

Adult population worldwide: 4,985,000,000 people.

- 70.1 percent have equity of less than $10,000.
- 91.4 percent have equity of less than $100,000.
- 0.7 percent have more than $1 million in equity.
- 87 percent of millionaires (those with more than $1 million in equity) have equity of between $1 million and $5 million.

Let's take a look at the global wealth pyramid 2017:[66]

Global wealth pyramid 2017

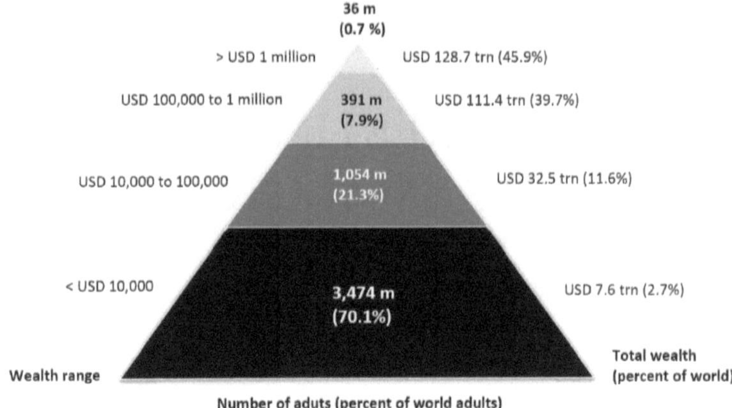

Source: James Davies, Rodrigo Lluberas and Anthony Shorrocks, Credit Suisse Global Wealth Databook 2017.

The top of the pyramid

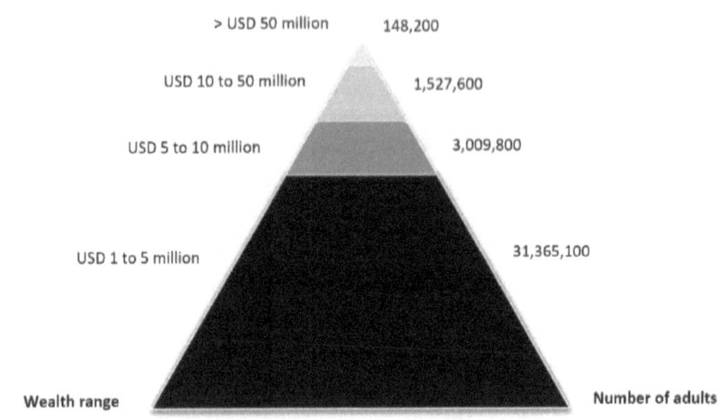

Source: James Davies, Rodrigo Lluberas and Anthony Shorrocks, Credit Suisse Global Wealth Databook 2017.

Median Wealth per Adult Ranking (in US Dollars)

1. Switzerland: $229,000
2. Australia: $195,400
3. Belgium: $161,000
4. New Zealand: $147,600
5. Norway: $130,500
6. Italy: $124,600
7. Japan: $123,700
8. France: $119,700
9. Singapore: $108,900
10. United Kingdom: $102,600

    ...

21. United States: $55,900

These charts are very important so you can understand how significant the following analysis is. Without having data on the finances of the world's population, it might seem that people have much more money than they really do. In this mix is the fact that many people you know have much higher expenses than they can really afford.

Many people think about how much they should spend on an item in relation to their income. The most extreme cases may involve seeing if their bank balance at a specific moment is enough to make a particular payment. Worse than that, some just look to see if there is some space for additional spending in the credit line of their card.

Consider the first example, which is very common. This is not the way it should be done. According to the book *The Millionaire Next Door*,[67] there are many people with very high incomes but low equity and vice versa. Those with high income/low equity usually have high-level educations from good/excellent universities, live in expensive cities, and have a very high lifestyle. They earn a lot and spend a lot but don't invest a lot; consequently, they have little equity. Taking this approach in life is very risky, since incomes are temporary and can go from six or seven figures to zero in the blink of an eye. The other problem is that it's easy for a person to upgrade their lifestyle but very difficult to downgrade it. When someone upgrades their way of living, in a few months or less, they take that type of living for granted, and that is the new base. Keeping this data in mind, if their income suddenly goes to zero, their life is going to be miserable because downgrading hurts.

For a more conservative approach, every expense in life should be considered in relation to equity. Even though equity can also decrease in value, it's much more permanent if you have a good balanced investment portfolio. Someone might receive the bad news of suddenly having no income (income from salary, not from equity gains), but if all financial decisions were made in relation to equity, the person is going to be in a much safer position. I'm simplifying to analyze the decisions in terms of equity to make a point. There are many things to consider when someone decides to purchase something, such as how averse to risk the person is, how much the person spends a year on average, what their saving capacity is, their personal tastes, their life expectancy, their earning capacity, whether they expect to leave an inheritance to their kids or to someone else or prefer to leave none, and other options.

Having a coffee every day in the regular coffee shop? "Why not? it's something I deserve." A cup of red wine every night with my meal? "Sure, it's great for my heart." (It's still controversial whether or not that's true,[68] so better stick with, "I like it.") "What do you mean, I am the one who should clean the house? Are you nuts? That's the maid's job."

Well, every small expense seems to fit into one of two categories: "It's just a few dollars; those few dollars are not going to change my financials," and "Those are things that make life worth living, and I can afford them." Well, those two reasons, at least for 92 percent of the world's population (the ones with less than $100,000 in equity) are totally wrong.

People should think about every expense in their life in this way: if it's going to be a periodic payment, don't calculate it as one payment; think of it as a yearly total. If, for example, you ask the price of a gym membership and are told it's $120 a month, automatically think, OK, $1,440 a year. Then do the following thinking: OK, I'm going to go to this gym for at least five years; that's $8,591. It's not the $1,440 multiplied by five years. It's that plus including interest payment opportunity. (No need to do it mentally; use a financial calculator). Use the annual rate you'd be earning if you put that money into stocks of the Standard and Poor's (S&P) 500 index, for example, instead of joining the gym. Neither is better or worse; it depends on what you like, what makes you happy, and most important whether you can afford it in relation to your equity (not your salary income, which is temporary).

The S&P return is approximately 10 percent. That has been the average annual return since its inception in 1928 through 2017.[69] In most future cases in this book use a return of 7 percent, which is a more conservative and realistic approach. If we adjust inflation to the S&P index, the return is around 7 percent.

With expensive items, the numbers are so clear that you don't even have to pull out your financial calculator. If your equity is $70,000 and you are planning to purchase a $7,000 Hermès bag, you don't need to pull out your financial calculator, that payment definitely doesn't make sense. This is nothing new; most rational people think this way. This doesn't mean that there are a lot of irrational people. Most luxury brands aren't targeted to millionaires. Well, maybe the target is millionaires and for aspirational buyers, but the real buyers are not millionaires. As pointed out in *The Millionaires Next Door*, most luxury brands are purchased by superrich people or by people who aren't millionaires but want to look like they are. Worldwide, millionaires with equity in the range of $1 to $5 million (who, as we saw, account for 87 percent of those with more than $1 million) are not the ones consuming these luxury brands in general. Most of their clients are those with less than $1 million in equity who, by definition, are not millionaires.

So, let's crunch the numbers. (In these cases, price increases are not going to be considered. A different exercise could be done setting an estimated price increase based on the historic price increases of that item or service, subtracting that from the rate that could be earned from the S&P index (the 7 percent previously mentioned). Doing that would more precisely determine the value of money in time. Those considerations, however, are not part of this exercise, which aims to put things simply. (See Appendix J).

A house cleaner working an eight-hour-per-day schedule will cost you around $6,500 a year in some Latin American countries. The monthly payment is $542. Over twenty years, the house cleaner will cost $282,170 (opportunity cost). Over thirty years, it will be $660,822. In other words, not having a house cleaner for thirty years will make you $660,822 richer. Not bad for dedicating a few hours a day to cleaning and cooking.

Some people calculate how much they earn per hour (say, one hundred dollars), and if hiring someone to perform the service will cost eight dollars an hour, they analyze it this way: "My time is much more valuable than the cost. Why should I weed the garden when it costs me eight dollars an hour to have someone else to do it, and an hour of my work is valued at one hundred dollars?"

A lot of articles say that it's better to spend on things that save you time so you can use that time on the things that you really want or love, such as spending quality time with your kids.

As a concept this sounds good, but it's not practical for most people. The $282,170 you can save in twenty years by not having someone clean your house is more than what most people end up saving for retirement. So the concept is good as long as you can afford it, but most people in the world can't afford to reduce their retirement funds by $282,170.

Many things sound good as concepts but are applicable to very few people. You can say that it is a great idea to hire a chauffeur so instead of wasting your time in your daily driving commute, the chauffeur can drive, and you can focus on what you really want or love; reading, working on your laptop, watching a movie or sleeping a little bit more. Well, sounds nice, but again, only if you can afford it.

How about that daily Starbucks? The average price of a tall cappuccino in the United States is $2.75. That is $42,976 over twenty years or $100,648 over thirty years. One great reference is comparing this to a premium Italian coffee bean and the required milk for making that cappuccino at home or at work. This cup will cost you $0.40. If you make this switch (which, by the way, wouldn't sacrifice quality, as Starbucks' cappuccino is very poorly made) you will end up being $36,725 richer in twenty years or $86,008 richer in thirty years.

One of the most nonsensical consumptions is cigarettes. Using the average price of a pack in the United States, which is $7, doing the same exercise, you'll end up $109,395 richer in twenty years and $256,194 in thirty years based on regular smoking habits.[a] You will also live ten years longer on average and not spend tens to hundreds of thousands dollars that lung cancer treatment can cost.

Let's do the same exercise with kids' expenses. As previously stated, it cost $233,000 to raise a kid from zero to eighteen years old in a middle-class family in the United States. That translates to $1,079 each month, so you'll end up $464,620 richer in eighteen years (with two kids, it's $929,241, and so on).

Now let's combine these three things. This is a lazy guy who hates cleaning his house, is a coffee and cigarette lover, and has two kids. Bottom line: $1,363,782 in twenty years (eighteen years for the kids).

There's a bonus story: makeup. It wasn't included with the examples above; you'll soon know why.

The cosmetic industry is a $130.7 billion per year business.[70] They are selling an illusion. An illusion that has been a great business. Many women use makeup to increase their self-confidence, to look younger, to look prettier, to find

---

[a] It considers one pack (20 cigarettes) daily.

a possible mate, to keep their mate, and to compete with other women. These are the motives that drive them to use makeup. But is makeup cheap? It might look cheap, depending on the brand. If you look at it in terms of each time women purchase it, it may seem affordable, but putting all that money together as in the coffee example above is a totally different matter. There's a study of the US market that puts an average value to a woman's face: how much it cost a day on average, for all the products a woman uses. This amount is eight dollars.[71] (It's a little surprising that 85 percent of the women in the study used an average of sixteen skincare and cosmetic products every day.)

This eight-dollar cost comprises into five dollars on skincare products and three dollars on makeup. Well, somebody will say, "OK, if it's for self-confidence and beauty, it's OK to spend that three dollars on makeup. Better to invest that daily three dollars than to die alone!" Not so fast…

Again, that intuition doesn't work. Women may be overestimating the power of makeup. It is useful for the purposes mentioned, but not at the amounts they are using the products. After a study that took photographs of several women (normal people, not top models) wearing different degrees of makeup ranging from 0 percent to 100 percent, it was discovered that men preferred women wearing much less than 100 percent makeup. Men preferred women with 50 percent of full makeup, and they rated those wearing no makeup better than those wearing 100 percent.[72]

Taking all this insight into account, it's a better option for a woman to invest less in makeup: at least half of what they are investing now. That means $1.50 instead of $3. So it sounds like a good choice to invest $1.50 less daily, while enhancing her attractiveness to the opposite sex.

Here is why I didn't combine this with the examples above. In the specific example, a twenty-year period is too short to consider. If women start to use makeup around the age of fifteen, under no circumstances would they stop using it at thirty-five. That's the moment when they start to use even more makeup, because they want to mask signs of age. So, realistically they can wear makeup for a fifty-year period. There is no available study of how much they use by age or how long they use it. But for this example, fifty years seems reasonable. Not considering inflation and with a 7 percent investment rate, in fifty years the savings will add to $245,163. Not bad for being prettier and having an extra $245,163 in your account at age sixty-five.

Lesson learned: just do the math.

## CHAPTER TEN

UNDERESTIMATING OUR SELF-CONTROL

Have you ever heard that gyms are full of new members in January? That's because people feel an obligation to go to the gym, maybe because of New Year's resolutions. If they have already paid for the full year, they feel the urge to use it. The same is true for retirement funds. People want to pay for someone searching for them to make the periodic deposit. If not, they'll pay a penalty. On average, retirement funds end up earning at best the same as the market in the long run, so why don't you just play the market (put your money in an ETF like an S&P 500 index) and avoid giving explanations to the financial advisors, meeting deadlines, and more stress in your life? That's because you pay someone to put pressure on you. Many people act like children and need to pay for someone (in this case, the fee that charges the retirement fund) to keep an eye on their discipline.

The other common obligatory expense many people have is real estate. In the same way, people like to feel the pressure of the monthly payment instead of putting that money in their investment account, even though, in the long term, the stock market on average has performed far better than real estate. People don't trust themselves and feel that if they have too many liquid assets, they won't be able to control themselves, and they'll end up spending everything they have and more.

Is it smart to do these things? Well, avoiding the most annoying answer "It depends", the right answer is that you should choose one of these things (gym, retirement fund, or real estate) if you think it's a good alternative in your life among all the choices you have. You should pay for the gym in January (or in any month) only if you really enjoy gyms; it's near your home or office so it won't be a pain every time you commute there; and it's a better alternative for working out than running in the park, playing tennis, or participating in a similar activity. Consider also if the membership fee makes sense in your budget. To know if the retirement fund is the right choice, you should consider first if the company in which you are putting the money is professional and trustworthy. If you are going to put a certain amount in it periodically for around twenty or thirty years, it's very important to do the necessary homework and know you can trust that company; it is not like buying lunch.

As for buying or renting the house you plan to live in, the smart choice is to know if, in that specific area, it is better to rent or to buy. It's not difficult to calculate that. First, calculate the annual rent divided by the estimated value of the property. For example, you have $1 million cash. There is an apartment for rent for $2,000 a month ($24,000 a year), and the property's value is $1 million. That means you are paying 2.4 percent a year. That is a very good option. In that case renting is better than buying. If you have $1 million and invest it in the stock market, it will make an average return of 8 percent a year in the long run. So, in this case, it is better to invest the $1 million, earn $80,000 on your investment, pay $24,000 in rent, and reinvest the other $56,000 in the market. It would be a very bad idea to purchase that apartment.

On the other hand, if the rent is $8,000 a month ($96,000 a year), you would be paying 9.6 percent of the property's value. The same $1 million investment will only give you around $80,000 a year, so you'd be better off buying the apartment and saving the $16,000 (the difference between $80,000 and $96,000 in rental cost). This exercise should be done with more detail, but it's a brief example of how the logic works.

In the second example, you don't have that $1 million in cash. You just have $50,000. This time you need to look for a loan of those $950,000. Let's say that you find a loan with a 6 percent interest rate. You'll pay $57,000 a year in interest alone. You must pay not only interest but also capital. To make it simple, just considering the interest, in this case it is better to pay the $24,000 in rent and invest the remaining $33,000 (or all the $50,000 you started with) (assuming you can afford $57,000 for housing, which is why you are considering a $950,000 loan and paying $57,000 in interest in the first place).

In the third example, as in the previous one, you are asking for the loan because you don't have the $1 million. You just have the $50,000. In this case, the rent is $96,000. Considering the $57,000 of the loan's interest of the $950,000 is a good idea, purchasing is a good deal.

In the cases of purchasing the property, you should also consider the amount you can deduct from your taxes when you invest in real estate, but, for reasons of simplicity, that is not considered here. This examples also not consider the property appreciation or depreciation, which is very difficult to estimate due to many variables.

These examples are the most objective possible. Paying for a gym membership for a year just to feel the pressure to go even if you don't like working out in a gym that much. Or paying high management fees for a retirement fund so you're pressured to save. And one additional pressure: paying back the bank loan before you spend that money on vacations.

Here's a good idea if you like to go to the gym. The sooner you do it the better; it is not a significant amount of money, but it is a smart choice.

Maybe it isn't a bright idea to pay for a gym membership. (Some people love working out in a gym, packed with commercial equipment, so this wouldn't apply to them). How about creating your own gym? Think about whether there's enough space at your home for your own gym. If so, all you need to do is purchase the equipment. The problem for the gym lover is not that pressure mentioned above, but the gym's opening hours. If your commute is long and you want to work out a lot, maybe around 4:30 a.m. is a good time to do your routine. The problem is that most gyms open at 6:00 a.m., so, you'll end up doing an incomplete workout and being in a hurry all morning. In summary, you'll pay for a service but won't be satisfied.

Using those numbers, the result is the following:[b]

The equipment costs $4,000. (See Appendix K). You'll use 12 square meters of your home for the gym. Those 12 square meters cost $70 (rent price). Take the breakeven in a decent

---

[b] Considering home equipment and not a complete gym—just some basics for your daily routine. The prices vary by location. The purpose is to think about the logic of the exercise.

amount of time: five years. Four thousand dollars' worth of equipment over five years means $94.50 each month. Adding $70 for the space is $164. That's around the gym's monthly payment. While you are only paying for five years, you'll end up using that gym for twenty years. So, from year five and one month, you'll only be paying the rental cost, $70.

There are additional benefits. You can use the gym twenty-four hours a day. You won't have to deal with someone else's sweat, listen to annoying people screaming due to the tremendous weight they are benching, watch TV programs you don't like, listening to terrible music, or use nasty showers. (Even though they aren't necessarily nasty, it's all in your mind). The worst part of all is waiting for someone to finish using a machine. At home you decide your style, your music, your TV programs, and your schedule, and you can use the machines all day long if you want to. It sounds like a total win.

The takeaway here is the numbers. It might sound like a good idea to compromise money that limit your cash flow so you won't spend in worthless things all your money. But financially speaking, it's a terrible idea. Better to control your impulses; if not, the price paid for those impulses can be quite high.

## CHAPTER ELEVEN

UNDERRATING "BUYING EXPENSIVE"

Walmart is the king of cheap things. Maybe that explains why it is the world's number one company in revenue[73]. It was once also the king of retail (market capitalization) until Amazon, another company that loves breaking prices, took the lead (retail companies). It's not that Amazon is what it is today because of its cheap prices; it has enormous advantages that are very difficult to replicate, and recently, it has turned into such a big company and has so much money and so many great ideas that it's difficult for anyone to compete with it. Even though it has many advantages, one of the things that has made it grow is having the best prices. Amazon lost money for about twenty years, mainly to become the consumer's preference when they want to purchase online, first with books and now in 2019, with almost anything. It captures consumers mainly by having the most competitive prices in the market, but also with amazing service, a great shopping experience, great delivery, and being a trusted place to use a credit card, among other things.

Price is subjective. No item is cheap or expensive by itself. The obvious way to know if a price is high or low is comparing it to the price of something similar. There are items among which the difference is minimal, so a difference in cents might make you go for the cheapest one. There is another type of items that might look extremely expensive, but some people are ready to pay for it—not necessarily because they are rich but, in many cases, because the cost/benefit produces a good deal. Some Amiri jeans for $1,000? There are people who go crazy for them. Many people wouldn't wear them even if they got them for free. The point to consider is that the value someone places on an item is very personal. Besides being personal, there are businesses that have done great marketing and transformed consumers in such a way that they are willing to pay a lot of money for certain items. They have captured a substantial number of people willing to do this, and that's why these companies survive for many years making money. Think about Tiffany & Co., Rolls Royce or Chanel. They all sell upscale luxury at a premium price.

Whether people decide to buy cheap items or luxury items, they like to get the best deal on those items. In the example above, some consumers of Amiri jeans may hunt for the very best price, and if they find the $1,000 jeans for $800, they'll feel it's a great deal. The wiser people are, the better the deal they want to get. It doesn't matter if it is a low-cost item or a luxury one. People like the best deal possible. There is a quote that says something like this, "Regular people like paying cheap; millionaires love it."

As mentioned before, it's important to think of periodic expenses on a yearly basis. Do the same when buying items. Many items may still be into the category of "periodic."

Periodic payments are usually considered the ones that you pay every month and in some cases every year (such as taxes). The trick for getting that great deal that everyone loves is putting every item in the periodic category. For example, for a serious runner, running shoes have a periodicity of around four months. Fancy, high-quality leather shoes have a periodicity of ten years. A good canvassed suit might last at least twice as long as a fused suit. A high-quality pair of glasses can last ten years easily; the cheap version will last no more than two years.

The problem with this strategy is that it is not easy to know how long an item will last if you haven't previously bought it. There might be recommendations but it's not easy to trust them because they always say, "It depends on how much you use it and if you take good care of it." With years of experience, you can become aware of how long an item lasts in terms of functionality and if you still like it.

In the case of the running shoes example, the quality of the shoe doesn't necessarily make it last longer than other shoes. The quality and high-performance shoes last around four months, the same as any entry-level running shoe. Here the difference is how comfortable they are, how well they protect your joints while you're running, and weight (for speed), among other factors. So here, purchasing a shoe costing $60 or $250 will not extend the use. (The only thing that might happen with the $60 shoe, even though it doesn't last longer, there's a higher probability that you can get your knee or joints injured, so it's better not to go cheap on this).

In the case of fancy leather shoes, there is a big difference. Besides comfort and esthetics, a good professionally made leather shoe costing about $500 or more (perhaps a Goodyear type) can easily last ten years, even if you use them with high frequency. Compare this to the cheap leather shoes, sold by Zara for around $80: first, they are very uncomfortable and second, they will last around one year in good shape. So the annual cost of the fancy shoe is $50 while the yearly Zara payment is $80. Which is the smarter choice?

People in general don't do this easy exercise. One of the reasons they don't is because of cash flow. Even though the first pair of shoes costs just $50 a year (less than the yearly payment for the Zara shoe), you must pay ten years in advance ($500). Because of this, it is very important to always have cash with you. If you don't have enough cash, as in the case with most of the US population, it is impossible to making smart decisions. Cash is indispensable to making smart decisions. There is an expression used in finance and when talking about investments: cash is king. This is very useful to keep in mind.

A lot of people spend on housing much more than they can easily afford.[74] They spend the maximum on it and don't leave themselves the capacity to get even a coffee during the month without getting stressed. Doing this will make them underestimate "buying expensive" because they're always out of cash. Financially smart people wear cool premium shoes for the price of cheap Zara shoes.

Talking about shoes, this item doesn't have the following problem: once you're an adult, your shoe size rarely changes.

People tend to get heavier as they get older, until around fifty-five years old for men and sixty-five for women, when they start to lose weight again.[75] How about purchasing a $6,000 Brioni coat but then suddenly gaining weight, so you can't wear it anymore? Here is when many people will say, "It's exactly like the gym membership!" That is the point I want to make. For those who like paying the gym membership in January or paying high fees for their retirement fund, this alternative sounds smarter. Not exactly buying a $6,000 Brioni coat, that might be out of the league of 95 percent of the world's population. That is just one example. Let's say buying a $2,000 suit. With this choice you get the urge to keep working out and eating healthy if you don't want to lose your investment. Making this $2,000 investment will help you stay fit and healthy while looking cool.

On the other hand, there are investments that don't add much for the extra money they cost. In a hotel you can upgrade or book a better room directly. Paying extra for the view in a spot with amazing views sounds good. How about paying an extra 50 percent to upgrade to a suite in which the only difference is having a sofa you barely use? Well, you use it to leave your daily dirty clothes on when you put on your pajamas. Putting your dirty clothes in a two-hundred-dollar spot of your room doesn't sound like a good deal.

It may sound that buying cheap is an obvious reason for being aligned in your goal of increasing your equity. That common sense is wrong. Buying cheap can lead you in a vicious circle in which you keep buying stuff. In the end you end up spending more and therefore not increasing your equity in an ideal way. The logic part here is how much the product you're buying will last and for how long you'll still like it. Then take it to a yearly basis, and there's more clarity on which option to choose

## CHAPTER TWELVE

UNDERRATING FINANCIAL FREEDOM

Several studies have been done on how many people actually like their jobs. A Gallup study said that 67 percent of the US workforce is "disengaged."[76] There's another set of data from LinkedIn saying that 80 percent of LinkedIn users don't like their jobs.[77]

Let's suppose someone is in that 80 percent of people who don't like their jobs. We can deduce from this figure that most of the people in this category are only working for the money, so if they had enough money, they wouldn't be there.

A great idea to end the torture of going more than forty hours a week to a job you hate is to gain financial freedom as fast as possible but in a safe way. That doesn't mean that people should be risky with their investment portfolios but do it fast and avoid high risk. Doing it safely means getting returns of 8 percent, which is a little less than the historic long-term returns of the S&P 500 index. It's not as easy as it sounds because it depends on when you buy and when you sell. You can lose a lot if you suddenly need money, and you need to sell when is not the right time. It is better to avoid that risk and always have a security fund for those urgent withdrawals.

There are basically three ways of creating equity: earning more, spending less, and earning more plus spending less. It may sound a little obvious that it is always better to earn more, but it's much more difficult. In that case you are dealing with something you don't have. The decision is not totally in your hands. There is a quote from *The Millionaires Next Door*: "It's much easier in America to earn a lot than it is to accumulate wealth."[78] I'm not sure that statement is correct. I'm confident it is not true for places outside the United States, but talking about the United States, it is subjective. How much is earning "a lot," and how much is "wealth"? Data from the *Wall Street Journal* (more up to date than in *The Millionaire Next Door*), indicates that the percentage of people earning less than $100,000 a year is 92 percent.[79] So saying that it is easy to earn a lot is wrong; $100,000 a year is not a lot, and if it were easy, more than just 8 percent of people would be earning more than that.

That research is great and surprising. People think that millionaires usually live like rock stars, but really that's far from the truth. Maybe it is the case for the richest millionaires, people who are worth more than $100 million, but not for the people who have less than $3 million in equity, who of course are still considered millionaires and who are the vast majority of the millionaire group. In conclusion, to be superrich, you need to have a high income. It's practically impossible to achieve this just by being a big saver with a low income. This will get you to the point of creating some equity but not in the millions range. On the other hand, whether you have a high or low income, it is necessary to be a big saver. If you focus on being a high earner but not on saving, you can easily end up with zero. That's the case of many professional athletes who earn millions when they're active, but when they retire, their fortunes don't last long.

Saving is easier than earning because you are dealing with something you already have. It's totally in your control how much you spend.

People in general are very bad at saving because they prefer to live in the moment rather than thinking about the future. Here's one tricky part. It's totally convincing, that concept of living in the moment, as Eckhart Tolle says in his bestseller *The Power of Now.*[80] The only certain thing in life is "now": why waste your time regretting the past or having anxiety about the future? Just enjoy the now, because there is happiness in having the joy of the moment. Applying the "now", if doing it correctly, isn't as difficult as it looks. Maybe this is the best philosophy to apply in life. It's very practical. It is not what most people do, which is enjoying the now, using up the last dime they have and thinking that maybe they'll die tomorrow. Better enjoy now, which means using all their worth plus racking up some debt. ("Why not? The credit card lets me.") It's not smart to trust what the credit card allows you; what the credit card really wants is for you to be in debt for the rest of your life. Doing that is completely misunderstanding the concept of living in the now.

Living in the now is enjoying the moment as it is. It can be a good moment, a regular moment, a boring moment, any type of moment. If it is on the positive side, just enjoy it. If it's on the negative side, you should deal with it right away. You shouldn't delay anything because you are dealing with that problem right now. It doesn't mean that to enjoy the now you don't have to think that there is an extremely high probability that there will be a tomorrow (remember, women in Japan are dying at eighty-seven years old on average)[81], so you'd better be able to afford food tomorrow. It is not indulging right now. It's enjoying humble things, free things now, things you can afford now, and making a safe nest for the worries of tomorrow. It would be better that tomorrow you deal with positive moments rather than the negatives as not having enough money.

How could someone in their right mind say something like "I prefer to enjoy each day as it comes because you never know what will come tomorrow or soon"? They say, "I don't know if I'll die tomorrow; what will I do then with all the money in the bank? Why should I be living a life of restrictions when I'm not sure how long I'll last?" Well, as stated before, there is a high probability that this person will live at least seventy-two years, so they would be better off not betting in a poker game trying to enjoy today because they are terrible at the probabilities game.

Here is where people underestimate their life expectancy, their financial freedom, how much and how long they will save in their lives, and how long that money will last.

The life expectancy data from the World Health Organization (WHO) 2015[82] gives a world average of 71.5 years old. The range starts in countries in Africa where the life expectancy is in the fifties and goes up to eighty-three in some developed countries.

Most of these people want to enjoy every day living the moment to the fullest but don't have a clear life philosophy. They think that a great percentage of their happiest moments are achieved with money. Money is the thing everyone is searching for, and their lives are restricted if it's scarce. People are used to enjoying things that can only be secured with money. The things that are free, such as breathing fresh air, walking in the park, or sleeping nobody cares about; they take them for granted. They want things that can be purchased with money. The contradiction here is that money is scarce, so if you spend it too fast, or at least faster than you can earn it, you'll end up with nothing. At that point they must learn to enjoy those moments they used to take for granted and not enjoy, like a walk in the park, watching the sunset, or listening to the birds singing.

If people were to enjoy activities that don't require as much money from the beginning, it would be easy to have financial freedom early in life. Not necessarily earning top salaries but sufficient salaries and focusing on saving a lot. This is possible if you don't have expensive tastes to cover every day. If you are constantly in search of luxury items or other things you can't easily afford, it is extremely difficult to reach financial freedom. This way life will be a constant pain. Life without fulfillment. It doesn't have to be like that. Fulfillment in life comes from enjoying activities that develop your brain, your body, and your soul. It is usually not necessary to spend much money to enjoy those activities.

It's often true that you need to study in a formal institution if you want that good salary that'll bring you to early financial freedom. It is also true that education is one of the things that has been affected by inflation more than others. Regrettably, there's not much you can do about that, and education is something you should spend money on. There is a range of prices for every type of wallet, and it's something you should focus on early in life. After formal education, if people continue focusing their lives on activities that involve brain, body, and soul, the financial freedom will soon come. One way to save is to keep yourself busy. (Busy in terms of thinking and creating something, not busy shopping.) The busier you are, the less you spend.

People should be busy with an activity they have decided to engage in, enjoying that "now" and having enough discipline to invest their monthly savings. This should be an activity outside your formal job because, as we saw, it's estimated that 80 percent of people hate their jobs; the focus here is on this group. So the plan should be to do well at your job even if you don't like it, save, invest, achieve financial freedom, and do all this while participating in an activity you enjoy outside the office that doesn't involve spending very much.

All tastes are acquired. You were not born with them. You started to like things depending on what surrounded you. Maybe when you were very young, you didn't have the control or independence to decide what you liked. If you set your priorities straight, you can start separating ideas into different "baskets." In one basket, put the things that you got used to liking but aren't worth the time or money you spend on them. In another basket, put the ones that fulfill you and are cheap or free. Focus on the second ones.

That doesn't mean you should forget the first basket. You can enjoy many of those things for free. For example, if you like paintings, you don't need to own a $100 million Picasso. You can just go to a museum, and many museums have a day on which admission is free. Another way to appreciate paintings is to buy a twenty-dollar book about the artist. Besides seeing the paintings, you can also go deeply into his or her story.

Do you like fancy architecture? You don't have to own it. I know that looking at a Norman Foster–designed house is not the same as living in one. But if you like architecture, you can get inspired by Foster's designs, investigate them, and go deeply into them, then hire an unknown architect to work on your crazy ideas. The end product will be many times cheaper than the Foster version and will be more fulfilling because you put part of yourself into it; you didn't just go out and buy it.

There is a reality that is quite strange: you love many items more when you don't have them than when you finally get them. Have you ever heard that a vacation starts when you begin planning it, maybe three months in advance? Many times, the planning is even better than the actual trip. Sometimes the trip doesn't go as expected: maybe the weather isn't good, the hotel that seemed great is terrible, et cetera. Even if you don't plan it, many times the knowledge that the trip is coming generates more happiness than the trip itself. This feeling is very common, and most people have experienced it. The point is that this also happens with material things. It is better to dream about that car you always loved, and the illusion of one day having it than to actually purchase the car. That ecstasy just lasts some months. Then you stop thinking about that car, and the new adventure of searching for another wish starts.

That doesn't mean you shouldn't buy anything of good quality. Remember the cost/benefit-on-yearly cost scenario? Yes, you should determine every expense in a yearly cost context and determine how long it will last. Most often, neither buying the cheapest nor the most luxurious will turn out to be the best choice. The cheapest won't last long, and the daily cost is very high while in the case of the ultra-luxurious, in many cases you are paying for an intangible, a feeling, a name more than quality. In this case the daily cost is very high because these items don't last much longer than a merely acceptable item.

Go for the good but not for the best. Usually the best deal is an item on the middle-high side. Many would say, "I know it doesn't last long, but I don't care. I want the style." In that case, it is better that you get the credits of the good taste and style more than the brand. While most luxurious brands show their logos, a great part of the credit will be attributed to the brand not to the user or owner. If someone sees you in a Porsche 911, they might think, "Porsche really makes nice cars," not "That guy in the Porsche has got great taste." Mm don't think so. There's nothing special in you in that supposed situation of "having style" owning a Porsche. It only relates to having the money to purchase that car, an attribute you can find in anybody with resources, and a car that you can find at any Porsche dealer. Everybody knows a 911 has great style; it wasn't your discovery.

It is different if, for example, you want to be different in terms of your clothing and accessories with no logo items. In that case the style is attributed 100 percent to the owner. That connection is easier to make with good but not extremely luxurious products, even though there are also superluxurious products with a no logo strategy. You will have style, originality, and some extra cash in your account.

Financial freedom is playing with the numbers, your tastes, and time (how long your money will last). What is a good number for financial freedom? Well, the math exercise is the other way around. The question should be what type of experiences and things do you want to purchase until the last day of your life, and approximately how many years you will you be alive?

Here are three variables to play with: the cheaper the tastes and the fewer the years you are expected to live, the less money you'll need. Move those three variables, and you'll reach the number you are searching for.

## CHAPTER THIRTEEN

OVERESTIMATING SHOWING OFF

Among all the behaviors each human being has, when considering their strengths, people tend to have one of these two: showing off or being humble.

Some people who are extremely good at what they do, extremely good looking, very charitable, and so on remain humble. The problem is that there are a lot of people who don't.

In terms of "things," it's clear that there are a lot of items that are well suited to being shown off. That's part of their success. Many luxury items play with that feeling. People want to show their success using specific brands. For example, take Louis Vuitton. This brand uses a style in its bags that is very well known; it states very clearly that the items are Louis Vuitton. They are covered with the "LV" logo or the complete words. If there is a purse that is not fully dominated by the logos, it has one very big logo, so everyone will see that the specific purse cost at least a two thousand dollars. (Well, it could be fake and cost just forty dollars, but that's a different story.)

There are some luxury brands that don't use the logo strategy and play the low-profile role. This type of brand usually attracts the very wealthy—people who don't want to show brands because they consider all that tasteless, so they purchase items because of the quality, style, and exclusivity.

Exclusivity means that few people have an item, and isn't easy to purchase. Some might say a Rolex Submariner is exclusive; well, it's not. (Talking about new models; vintage and collectibles are different story.) It's extremely easy to find, entry-level priced for a luxury watch, and has the highest market share in its segment. That means a lot of people have it. It isn't exclusive; it's just an everyday luxury.

Another reason the wealthy purchase no logo luxury items is that everybody knows they are rich, so they don't feel the need to show off.

Some brands play an in-between role. They don't have logos all over the product, but they have a specific design that is recognizable even though it doesn't say very much. Well, some of these items are only recognizable to the trained eye, and some are more universal. Think about Valextra (an Italian luxury bag and leather accessories company), which uses very subtle logos or no visible logo at all. It's also a brand that's not easy to find. That's what makes it unrecognizable to most people.

Hermès has a tie line whose design is made of small animals. It doesn't use any logo, but that type of design is very recognizable to a tie connoisseur. The same occurs with Bottega Veneta business bags that have no logo at all. Their woven leather design is their trademark.

There are two problems that all luxury brands must deal with: being profitable and lasting in time. For that, they must choose between two options, generally speaking. The first is growing sales. One choice is increasing points of sale; it can be in their own stores or through department stores, outlets, or alliances with other brands that have their own stores. A second choice in this strategy is to grow sales through selling more items at the actual points of sale. They can do this by using mass marketing and making people want their products or by discounting them through promotions.

The second option is not increasing the number of items sold but drastically increasing the price per item. If they don't suffer a decrease in items sold, the total revenue will increase.

Increasing the price per item drastically is something that is very difficult to do. Brands, once launched, get a perception in the consumer mind, which is very difficult to change. If the brand is in the mainstream market, moving it to the everyday luxury or extreme luxury market is not easy. The consumer has already established a price range in his or her mind for a specific brand. Upscaling it is almost impossible. On the other hand, downscaling is easy to do, although it maybe not be the wise option.

Since it is not easy to increase prices, most luxury companies choose the option of increasing points of sale combined with some sort of promotion to secure peak sales throughout the year. They combine this with launching some more affordable lines (for example, the Tiffany silver line) to reach more customers. On top of this, they start to include more and/or bigger logos to attract those clients who, through several studies, have said they love to show off these luxury brands.

Here is where the story starts…

People have been searching for status symbols for centuries. It might seem that it is something from these times, but it isn't.

For example, long pointed shoes were a status symbol in the Middle Ages. The reason was that these extremely long, pointed shoes were so impractical that they sent the message that the people wearing them didn't work (since it was difficult to work while wearing those shoes). It meant not working, not because they didn't have a job, but because they didn't need to work since they were rich. Lemons were also a status symbols in ancient Rome. They were very scarce and as a consequence expensive, and only a few could afford them.

In our day, these items have been replaced with luxury brands. The lemons of the past have been converted into the Dom Perignon of contemporary life. Both status symbols calm your thirst, your indulgence, or your desire to impress your friends.

Showing off seems to be part of everyone's life. It doesn't matter to which social class, country, or group the person belongs. Most people show off; what differs is the items they use. For example, a person from a low socioeconomic level shows off to their friends by serving meat at a party at their house. Meat is considered aspirational in the low socioeconomic class in Latin America—while billionaires might be showing off their private jets or yachts. Most people show off in their inner circle and with the people they compare themselves to.

There are also other things that aren't really "things" used for showing off. This category includes experiences like vacations spots, specific hotels, country club memberships, and playing an expensive sport such as polo or yachting. Another is showing off not with items but with million- or billion-dollar donations. If not, why is it that most if not all of these donations aren't anonymous? It's clear that the $45 billion that Bill Gates has donated so far[83] is to set an example to other billionaires to do the same. But besides him, if someone donates \$1 billion, we know he or she is a billionaire. Donating anonymously would be an even better way to make other people donate too. Kindness without vanity.

A third category that people brag about is talents. Being good at something is a reason for some to show off. That can be excelling at tennis, knowing history or art very deeply, speaking a foreign language, and so on.

Whether through a luxury item, a cool experience, or a talent, people tend to show off mainly to demonstrate success (financial/intellectual), gain acceptance, or show that they are better than others.

This concept is not the smartest approach someone can take. Instead of stimulating admiration, imitation or acceptance, in many cases it will provoke the opposite feelings. People are jealous and very competitive even though some might say they aren't.

Envy is a universal feeling that damages every type of relationship. It can be your wife, coworker, boss, cousin, basically anyone. It's a feeling that's difficult to measure because it is rare for people to accept or admit they feel this way. Even though envy will always be a negative feeling, some might be less bad than others. For instance, if someone envies the financial state of a friend, that person can work harder and smarter to attain the same perceived financial situation. ("Perceived" because you never know for sure what someone else's financial situation really is.)

Some things are attainable, and envy can be used as a motivation to reach goals. Another example may be envying the personal record that a friend gets in a marathon. It can motivate you to train, eat, sleep, and do everything better to match or improve on that record.

Envy is usually generated by people who are close to you. If you envy a celebrity, a billionaire, or an athlete, it is really admiration, not envy. Envy appears with those close to you who do better in a particular area. Since they are close to you, you feel that it is also possible for you to attain what they did, and you tend to think that you are doing something wrong, you have bad luck…any excuse you can imagine.

The worst part of envy is when it is focused on characteristics that are impossible to attain. For example, imagine someone is the close friend of King Felipe of Spain. If this friend were to envy him, there wouldn't be nothing he could do. He will never be the king of Spain, be part of the Borbón family or be six feet six inches tall. That envy will only destroy the person's self-esteem and make him sick.

The person who is envied is the one who usually is in a different kind of disadvantage. Instead of generating envy, it is better to avoid the situation in which people envy you. Envy can be generated even if you don't do anything. If a friend envies you because you are good looking and have a high success rate with women or men, there isn't much you can do. On the other hand, there are some areas in which you are in control, and it will always be better to keep low profile, hiding information that would generate that feeling. Generating envy will only get you into trouble. Being humble about your qualities will make your life much easier. You can have amazing things but try to have them in secret. It's critical, at least until you reach one big goal.

It's like Amazon when it was in its period of growth. It was very humble, out of the loop, attaining no profits for twenty years. Nobody was aware of the monster that was growing and growing, gaining extremely loyal customers and entering new categories and industries all the time. By the time everyone realized that Amazon could be a threat, it was too late. It had started selling just books, a humble strategy that no one cared about. It was the first element they used to start its consolidation as the market leader. It changed the book industry, and from there it started to change every industry it competed with. The industry it will end up destroying is the logistics industry. It doesn't seem like a good idea to have DHL or FedEx stock nowadays.

The point is, the company acted as an invisible force, carefully thinking about each step it took, sending the message that it was not that important without anybody noticing they were disrupting big industries.

The same should be the case with the attitude you have toward your attributes. Particularly at your job, avoiding the feeling of envy is very useful, and it will help you climb the corporate ladder. In most positions in a company, people can't do their jobs by themselves. There are few professions in which you don't need help from others. If someone is an artist, a writer, or an individual professional athlete (among other professions), they can basically do it themselves with some help. An athlete needs a coach and a trainer; a writer or artist needs a publisher and an art dealer respectively, but these are not the core part of those professions. The main part is their talent; those supports are extras. For those supports you won't need much of a strategy if you possess the talent. If you have a great individual talent, good for you; take advantage of it. On the other hand, if you are like most people who need a job in a company, you can be good, but there are thousands or millions who are as good as you; it's important to master the "envy strategy."

People can usually be envious of their peers, direct reports, and bosses.

Your peers are the most critical ones. Peers are your direct competitors. These are the ones with the highest possibility of being promoted to that position you dream of having. They are the ones competing for the same position, so they are the ones you must be the most aware of. From your first day at work, your relations to your peers should be very strategic. You should have them close to you but not so close that it generates a problem. Being helpful and nice is the basic approach. Delimiting clearly each one's responsibilities is very important. Most problems occur when a peer wants to interfere with your decisions without having the authority to do so. You should keep the boundaries crystal clear. The common attitude toward generating envy from your peers will only make your everyday life miserable and your promotion more difficult to get.

The more envy you generate, the less your peers will cooperate in common projects and the more they will do to make you commit errors, gossip about you, invent things, or change stories. Is it smart to have this psychological war just because you show up at the office with a South of France tan? (The quality of the tan doesn't tell where you got it, so this is assuming you tell where you got it). Showing up at the office with a $20,000 watch? Even though it is counterintuitive, this sends the wrong message to your peers. Unwise people think these luxuries mean that you are rich when you usually aren't. Most rich people don't spend on luxuries. Having a $20,000 watch means having $20,000 less in your investment account. Most watches (with exceptions) don't count as part of your equity or do count as equity but usually are not good investments. So not having that watch means you are wealthier. Psychologically, they think that if you have a $20,000 watch you must have so much money that you easily can afford that luxury. Statistically, that is not the case; average millionaires won't spend on that. (The preferred watch brand of millionaires is Seiko,[84] which is in the $200 range approximately, not thousands). Wise average millionaires are not your peers at your office, so they don't know that.

If you like luxuries, hide them, or spend on those things that nobody can see. Buy an expensive painting and put it in your safe. Or go for a South of France tan but just say that you got it on the weekend in your garden. Don't buy anything with a logo. If you want to spend a lot on clothing, buy a tailor-made suit, and only you and the great connoisseurs will know what you're wearing. (Again, your peers at the office are not those great connoisseurs of a tailor-made Kiton). Go to that Michelin 3-star restaurant but please, don't post it anywhere.

At work, the more someone envies you, the more possible it is they will do something to prevent you from climbing the corporate ladder. You need alliances to grow, alliances to do your projects well, and alliances to have someone defending you when you are not there to defend yourself. At work you must be very strategic; the ones who rise in a corporation are often not the smart and hard workers. Those two things are important, but the most important are the connections you create with the people in the company—not just with the most important people but with almost anyone you must deal with. Remember that in companies there are usually 360-degree evaluations. That means that people in the higher, the same, and the lower ranks can rate you. You never know how a bad rating is going to hurt your career. (You'll never know because it's always confidential). So you'd better create great relationships while not generating envy from day one.

Status symbols have been around since ancient times; that doesn't mean you should use them. They cause envy in people close to you, and the more envy you generate, the more problematic your life will be. Intuition might say that showing off makes you more appealing to people, but using deep thinking on this, you we can see that it may appeal to some, but it comes with great downsides.

## CHAPTER FOURTEEN

OVER-ENTERTAINED PEOPLE

The world has divided what is entertaining from what is boring. In a clichéd way, a lot of activities as well as people are typecast as funny and entertaining or boring, a guy who doesn't know how to enjoy life.

The beer guy-type is considered very entertaining. It doesn't matter if he is a boring conversationalist, lacks an interesting point of view, or lacks creativity. He doesn't need to have any specific talent other than knowing how to take a glass of beer into his mouth. The only thing that matters is that he knows how to enjoy life because he goes out with his friends every week. It doesn't matter how macho he thinks he looks with a beer in his hand even though his testosterone level says the opposite.[85] It doesn't matter that beer makes him fat and depressed, due to the intrinsic characteristics of any alcoholic beverage. It doesn't matter that it dehydrates him; increases his blood pressure, which can lead to a stroke; and raises his triglyceride levels. And just to end his day as a hero, if he finds a sexy woman that night, he should get laid in a sloping bed to cope with his acid reflux and then afterward deal with insomnia. All this if he doesn't crash on his way home. It's hilarious that this beer guy believes in studies funded by alcohol companies that promote moderate drinking, which conclude that alcohol in small quantities is good for the health. Maybe what he doesn't know is that the scientists involved in that research are four to eight times more likely to conclude in favor of the sponsor of the study.[86]

There is another stereotypical guy: the "boring" one. Let's think of this guy as introverted, which is the most common type in this category. He is the one who likes to socialize but in a different way from the beer guy. He likes to do it in very small groups and not as frequently. When in a conversation, he likes to keep on the same topic for a long time until there's no more to say about it. If by accident, some new guy gets into the group that night, he will start a deep conversation, no small talk. Small talk might only be acceptable when they run out of important topics. When he decides to have a drink, he might have at most two, if he doesn't stick to just one. He is the healthy one who knows what he eats because he understands that his body is like a machine. He might say, "You don't put cheap gas into a Ferrari." He knows that if he wants his body and mind to perform at their best, he must put the best into his body. This is the kind of guy who has everything on a schedule. He loves routine. Routine is the quality that makes him outperform others in every aspect he competes in and makes him good at things he's interested in being better at.

This is a guy who might decline a lot of social plans. He does this because most of these invitations are not part of his routine. Trying to take him out of his routine makes him weigh up what's more important. For example, going out for some drinks while sacrificing eight hours of sleep? No way—he wants to be at peak mental performance in the next day's important meeting. Having some drinks and risk spending above his budget limits? One night of drinks with some new people isn't worth his attention because he estimates the high probability of not feeling engaged with that group. Going out for drinks because he might feel FOMO (fear of missing out, meaning that he is anxious about not going and missing something important there)? No way. This type of guy doesn't feel that regularly.

It might sound like the beer guy is enjoying the moment while the boring guy is not; he's only thinking long term. It's not really that way. The beer guy might be creating a network that can be useful in the mid- or long-term future. He's not enjoying just the moment he's drinking but the connections with people that could last a long time. There is a chance that those relationships created in the drinking process could give him great happiness in the long term. On the other hand, if those relationships aren't created, the joy would only be in the present moment, which is great. The problem is that in the mid and long term, serious health problems may appear; consequently, that guy will definitely not enjoy future moments, (Or, to be clearer, he will have to deal with more negative moments once they arrive.)

There is another problem here. People usually go out for a drink with the same friend or group of people. Those are drinking buddies. If that is the case, the supposed networking they might be doing isn't actually real. Even worse, it's very well known that, for example, for doing business or finding a better job, the ones who are the most useful are acquaintances, not close friends.[87] So if someone really likes going out for a drink, there are two good options. For enjoying the specific moment, going out with their drinking buddies is a great idea. If the purpose is searching for new opportunities in life, it's better not to stick with those drinking buddies and start creating new acquaintances.

The boring guy is doing both: enjoying the moment doing what he likes and somehow guaranteeing a joyful future. It may look like sleeping those eight hours is good and healthy; for the beer guy, it is a waste of time. He's the one that might say, "You'll have a lot of time to sleep when you're dead." For the boring guy, those eight hours of sleep have two aspects: the joy of enjoying a deep sleep and knowing that the next day he's going to be totally focused and strong in whatever he wants to do.

Here there shouldn't be much discussion because it is a matter of taste. The beer guy enjoys the moment with people and laughing; the boring guy enjoys the moment in activities he does alone or with a few people. The objective part that goes beyond tastes is that while both are enjoying their present moment in their own way, the beer guy is limiting his prospects of enjoying future moments. For example, he's not going to be focused at work the next day; he may be tired, have a headache, et cetera. Worse than that, if he exceeds in that type of entertainment it can lead to health, family, or work issues. The key part of the philosophy of enjoying the now is enjoying every single moment, not just the activities you like the most while damaging the future moments due to the poor selection of a specific activity in the present.

What is envy? The dictionary defines it as "Painful or resentful awareness of an advantage enjoyed by another joined with a desire to possess the same advantage."[88] In other words, people envy someone who is more successful than themselves in any area that is meaningful to them. If this is the case, envy doesn't exist toward someone who's a failure or has nothing special. That is why the more power a person gets, the more haters they generate. Power is created with great ideas, innovation and doing something in a better way. It's very common for people to be against change. There is resistance to innovative things, and the people driving these changes create a lot of hate in many cases due to envy.

Does someone whose passion in life is constantly going out for a beer have something special? Does someone require something special to be allowed into a bar? Is a beer so expensive that it's restricted for most of the population? The answer is a straight no. It requires no talent at anything. That's why nobody usually bad-mouths people who do that. Criticizing someone is almost always due to envy. There are exceptions. Maybe someone would criticize a homeless person, not feeling empathy with them and saying that the government should do something to eliminate them from the city. Others might criticize bad politicians or famous people. Many times, people don't criticize those they only know through media out of envy. Well, there are occasions when an average woman says, "Oh, Kate Moss is too thin," but it's clear what the purpose of that comment is.

More often, people criticize those close to them, rather than famous people. Family, friends, coworkers, bosses, acquaintances. Many times, this is because of envy. People like bad-mouthing others for different reasons, all revolving around envy but triggered in different ways. Sometimes it's because the criticized one is living a life much different from the rest, a type of life they like or the one they think they should be living. People love to criticize things that are different from what they have selected for their own lives. If the unfortunate object of criticism is a musician struggling in his starting years and suddenly having some success, people might say, "Oh, he's a loser. Look how this poor guy has wasted his life writing and playing songs nobody listens to. How is he going to raise a family in those poor economic conditions?" That opinion is worth nothing. Maybe the one doing the criticizing said that because he can't stand being at the office he hates for ten hours a day anymore and would prefer the flexible schedule of the musician. And what about a family? Why would he think that everybody wants to raise a family? Maybe that guy doing the criticizing is part of the statistic that says American parents are less happy than nonparents,[89] so, he desperately wants the aforementioned musician to be part of that statistic and as miserable as he is.

Because people make constant comparisons to their peers and close acquaintances, envy is an undesirable feeling that many people have. It is so negative and embarrassing that nobody wants to talk about it or admit that they have it. It's so undesirable that there is very little data about it.

A recent study of human behavior was developed by researchers from the Universidad Carlos III de Madrid with colleges from Universities of Barcelona, Rovira i Virgili, and Zaragoza.[90] It concludes by categorizing people into four groups depending on their personality type: optimistic, pessimistic, trusting, and envious. This categorization can be applied to 90 percent of the population. The most common was "envious" with 30 percent; the others were 20 percent each. The remaining 10 percent were people who, because of their personality type, couldn't be assigned to any group.

Many people accept that they are complicated, hysterical, liars, and have other negative defects possessed by humanity. But envy? That is so low that everyone prefers to avoid the topic.

There are two general preferences for every human being. That is being accepted by a group of people and to climb up or keep in a high social status during their lifetime. Being part of a group is something most can achieve. Most people have at least two close friends they can count on within the average of eight friends, so that part has been achieved by most. Social status climbing is a little more difficult. Most people die in the same socioeconomic status into which they were born. Climbing it's not an easy task.

Because of the difficulty of attaining that rise in social status, many people are desperate to obtain what they don't have. Since childhood, their parents have tried to live in the best neighborhoods, put them in the best schools possible, and send them to extracurricular activities to widen their knowledge, all with the sole goal of giving them the possibility of being part of the highest status possible. Placing them in the highest class possible improves their chances of having many more opportunities in the future. It's supposed (and it's true) that the highest class has access to better education, better jobs, more business opportunities, and more money, so it sounds smart to be part of this group.

Once children have gotten access to this select group, coexistence makes them similar to one another. People like to be part of groups. Usually there are different groups—for example, the group in the classroom, the musical group they are part of, a sports team, and others.

Trying to be part of that group, as with any group, requires some abilities. For most people they come naturally; they aren't forced. This is truer at a young age when kids are innocent and don't try to take advantage of the situation. This becomes different at an older age.

Empathy; identifying things in common; and having similar tastes, values, and hobbies while learning to have a good time together are things that generate trust within the group. That's when good friendships start. When kids start growing, they start to realize that it's cool to be friends with important, powerful people: in short, with great leaders, people who can increase your own chances of being successful too. Once kids become adults, they keep the same thing in mind. In general, if they have the chance, people would like to be friends with powerful people, politicians, celebrities, top athletes, famous artists, Fortune 500 CEOs, and so on.

When people have a big group of friends and acquaintances, they begin to compete with one another. They try to be in the best situation within the group because that is their point of comparison. They can measure whether they are doing well or not so well in life. As previously mentioned, this group, your close group in every activity you decide to do, is your point of reference for success. Nobody cares about the statistics. How well are top performers doing in the world in some activity? That is not important; people want to know how well they have done in life compared to their peers. There is enough data to validate this statement.

Here comes the contradiction in terms concerning how envy works. Would you like to be Mark Zuckerberg's close friend? Most would, definitely. So why is it that if someone starts climbing the corporate ladder while gaining more and more power and money, their friends and acquaintances start to feel envy? Why do people feel pain if a close friend or acquaintance is turning into the next Zuckerberg? Wouldn't having your friend turn into the next Zuckerberg be the same as being Zuckerberg's friend in the first place? Why does the first give you pleasure while the second gives you pain? It is clear in the analysis that you envy people who are close to you not so much strangers. People don't envy Zuckerberg; instead they feel admiration. The only ones who might feel envy are the people who are close to him.

The same thing happens with beautiful women. Research has discovered that they prefer to be friends with women as pretty as they are.[91] The point is why in the first instance they try hard to be part of the pretty group, and once there, bearing in mind that to be part of the group they are as pretty as the rest of the group, they start to feel envy. In this case that envy wouldn't be as much if they decided to be friends with the not-so-pretty group. That is not the case; they prefer to be part of the group of beautiful women expecting some upside but also the bad part that comes with envy.

Why would people like or try desperately to have friends who are in powerful positions, but only once these people have reached that status? When their close friends are on the road to reaching that status, they don't like it and prefer that these friends not reach success, at least not more success than they have themselves. So if someone becomes a new friend with a Fortune 500 CEO, how long will it take for that person to start feeling envy? Or will it never happen because they became friends with that CEO when he or she already had that status? Is it not the position but the change in status of that person that bothers the one feeling envy?

Let's get back to the boring guy. Is it possible that the beer guy or anyone else envies this guy?

Here are two hypotheses. First, if someone envies another person, then the second person necessarily should have something special in terms of being good at something or have some good qualities that are not easy to copy. A second hypothesis is that the more fulfilled a person is in different aspects of his or her life, the less envy he or she will feel toward other people.

It is clear, and many studies validate the common reasons why people envy others. Those are money, professional success, weight, physical attractiveness, relationship status (not being alone), fertility and children (in the sense of being able to have kids), and social media. Some of them are more common in men (a good career and money) while others are more frequent in women (weight, good looks, and fertility).[92]

What attribute does that boring guy have? He may have a lot of qualities. Lots of professions that require talent besides people skills are packed with introverts: artists, athletes, writers, inventors, musicians, and medical doctors, among others. All these professions require a lot of talent, focus, and time invested to be outstanding. He might not be as good at creating a network that translates into good opportunities; that's why extroverts earn around 10 percent more than introverts.

Wharton Professor Adam Grant did research that proved that in a profession such as sales, although extroverts are generally considered better, it isn't true.[93] They don't generate more money for a company than introverts do. This was to disprove the general view of corporations, which tend to give the most important positions to extroverts. This boring guy has one attribute that is the cause of envy in the beer-guy type:

independence. He can be very happy just with himself. That is an easier way to live because there won't always be people with whom to hang out. There can be times in life when it's possible to have people to get out with for fun. This is usually in their youth. Those drinking guys feel anxiety for the unknown future and scared of possible solitude they can't stand. That boring guy is lucky to enjoy himself. Isn't it better when enjoying your free time depends only on yourself? It's like trying to play a sport and deciding that basketball is the one you want to dedicate time to. It is not that easy to find nine other guys to play with. That type of match is frequently canceled. On the other hand, with running for example, you don't need more than a good pair of shoes and a good pair of knees. That's it. You can enjoy it anywhere, any day. Isn't it better not depending on others?

The best way to enjoy a hobby, besides having interest and some talent, is first to be consistent, so you'll get better at it. It is easier to stick with a hobby you are good at; when you are good at something, you can enjoy it more. That is the difficult road you must travel that'll make you stick with any sport. First you should pass that tough stage when you are really bad at it, when it's easy to get discouraged. Once you conquer that annoying part, you start enjoying it. It's practically impossible to enjoy a game you are not good at at all. If you go to play golf and you can barely hit the ball, you definitely won't like it. Or if you start running and you haven't yet reached the stage when nothing hurts, when you don't care if it's raining or it's 0 degrees Fahrenheit or 98. When you figure out that you don't need a timer, a GPS, a heart-rate monitor, music, or the most technically advanced clothing to do it without getting bored. If you haven't yet figured all those things out, it's going to be a nightmare.

The same goes with any activity. This boring guy doesn't deserve that name; he is anything but boring. Not depending on others to do any activity means that he is never bored. By himself, he finds a lot of things that he can do and enjoy doing. While the beer guy is desperate in his chat for having a get-together with his friends, the boring guy just takes a book, goes for a walk, or does some yoga. He can do it every day. Neither the extrovert nor the introvert personality is better than the other. But if life is enjoying every moment, even with the humblest things, that boring guy has a great advantage.

Most parents use intuition when educating their kids. Part of that is trying to make them develop an extroverted personality. With it, they will demonstrate confidence; they will (theoretically) be more interesting because they'll be someone who can be easily accessible for any type of conversation. They'll find a romantic partner easily and so on. That's not really the case. There is no such thing as molding your personality at that level. If someone is born introverted, there's not much anyone can do to make them extroverted and vice versa. Someone with an introverted personality has lots of strengths that are not clear without analyzing them. They have one downside that is not obvious either: they can cause envy in people. Envy generated by their abilities developed by focusing and not wasting time socializing.

Feeling envy doesn't make sense in a useful way. It may sound intuitive that you are OK because you're trying to "win," and winning is good, isn't it? The counterintuitive part is that friendship or being part of a group isn't a zero-sum game. All your peers to whom you compare yourself are enhancing you;

you're not losing. You're losing if you're envious. If you're part of that 30 percent of the population in the envious group, it is better to be treated. Not only because it's painful to live like that, but also because it's not smart.

If feelings of envy arrive, always have this question in your mind: Am I envious because the person I'm comparing myself to is in line to become more successful than I am, or because they have been successful since the day I met them? The answer to that question is "It doesn't matter; it's the same. Feel happy to have that friendship and enjoy it."

On the other hand, hanging around with people should have a limit. Time is precious and you need it to develop skills at and knowledge about anything. You might have the ability, but you need to spend time to perfect it. If you spend too much time hanging out and socializing, it will be very hard to be good at something.

## CHAPTER FIFTEEN

IS LAUGHING ENOUGH?

Laughing all day long is one thing; being happy is another. These two don't necessarily go together. Many people when depressed like to forget about everything with a get-together with someone who makes them laugh. That is a temporary relief for their depression. They forget for a moment about the deep problem that makes them feel bad and after a few hours return to their miserable state.

Initial laughter in any type of relationship is a sign of connection. There is some chemistry that feels good, and that's what anyone wants from a new friend, girlfriend, or boyfriend. The problem is that that first laugh might not last long. Other types of laughter might last longer, but are they fulfilling?

Initially, funny people can mask their real personalities. There are some who make you laugh at the beginning, but those laughs won't last long. The question is how to recognize the real personality of someone while not giving too much weight to how funny or entertaining they are.

Many people love to have a get-together with friends to release life's stress. It's a moment when everybody forgets problems while listening to countless repeated stories that still make you laugh. People are searching desperately for that space where all stress disappears.

The average person perhaps gives too much weight to fun when they talk about entertainment. Laughter and entertainment are not synonyms. What do you think was fun for Leonardo da Vinci? Maybe it wasn't listening every week to stories from his drunk friends. Laughs can be entertaining, but entertainment can also be 100 percent complete without laughs.

Usually people are labeled as boring if they don't laugh at meetings. There certainly are many ways of being entertaining. There are conversations in which too many laughs can be boring because usually they are very superficial. For someone who wants to deal in ideas, sometimes it's impossible to turn that conversation around. Funny conversations are not for everyone. Maybe the best type of conversations (as with reading) are the ones that have a mix. If a book is too serious, it feels like a textbook. If a conversation is too serious, it might feel like you are listening to a priest. On the other hand, if someone is too funny in a conversation, it might feel you are listening to Jimmy Fallon. Nothing wrong with Jimmy Fallon, he's great, but his monologues are good for twenty minutes, not for all night long.

Relationships are difficult. So difficult that 50 percent of marriages end in divorce. One of the main qualities that women look for in men is humor.[94] Women love men who make them laugh. Still, is it enough, those sparks from the beginning of the first date with continuous laughter until sunrise? Well…no. Woman tend to give so much weight to "lovely people" and not much weight to other things such as intellectual compatibility.

The usual story is the following: a woman dates a gentleman who makes her laugh all night long. While he is somewhat good looking, something she appreciates, they will end up having sex on average on their fourth date. For her, the summary at this moment is "He is funny, very entertaining, and we have sexual compatibility; this is meant to last." OK, let's wait a minute and give her a hand. This is just to prevent her being a part of that divorce statistic.

It's too cliché to say that beauty doesn't last long. Maybe beauty evolves, and people might be beautiful in a different way. It is not that someone in their twenties is more beautiful than someone in their fifties. It is not mathematical. It's more about what we have learned of what the term beautiful means to each of us. If not, don't they allow a fifty-year-old woman to be a contestant in the Miss Universe contest? Maybe it's because she's not going to be pretty enough to win under the standards we are used to.

Besides beauty, there has been a lot of searching for what makes a couple compatible. The most persuasive answer is that this happens when they are compatible in these areas: race/culture, religion, socioeconomic background, and intelligence.

Why do people want someone who makes them laugh? Maybe it is because most people usually think short term rather than long term. Why do people spend all the money they earn? Why do people overeat, catapulting the obesity rate to more than 30 percent and the overweight rate to more than 65 percent in the United States? Why are there so many smokers and drinkers?

All of them are thinking in the short term. "Let's enjoy a cigarette now; in the future I'll deal with lung cancer." "Let's spend all I earn on this vacation; if not now, when? When I get to seventy, I might not be able to travel anymore." "Don't be bored; eat this delicious dessert. Tomorrow you can run for a while to compensate for those calories."

It's quite strange that in these examples, we want things now. The curious thing is that we don't want everything now. How about "Why don't you vacuum the house?" "Why are you snoozing and ignoring the alarm clock? It's 4:30 a.m., running time." "Why don't you take the car to the carwash?" To all these questions people generally answer, "Maybe later or tomorrow."

When things are tough or boring, we want them tomorrow. When things are exciting, we want them now. When a guy is first dating a gorgeous woman and she asks, "How about having sex?" "Well, let's have it tomorrow." Mm, don't think so.

On one hand, humans are anxious; on the other hand, they are great procrastinators. The problem is that they are usually anxious for the things they should delay and vice versa. How is this?

From the example above: "How about having sex?" Procrastination would be a great idea. Wouldn't it be better to wait for some STD (sexually transmitted disease) test to avoid being one of those 357 million new cases each year?[95]

"Let's go shopping now." "Better wait fifteen days until the end-of-season sale starts." Another option would be "Wait until tomorrow. Just to stop for a moment and think if that is what you really want or if it's just a way to kill time and get over boredom." In both cases, better to procrastinate.

"Please press the snooze button again. I'll run tomorrow." Not a good idea to procrastinate here. The body starts losing muscle and getting out of shape in around two weeks. So better not to start that vicious cycle.

As in many examples in life in which people should start to change when they think about "now" or "some other day," the same applies to what they should do when in search of funny people, especially when it is a potential partner. Taking "now" that person who makes you laugh may be a pain if he or she converts into a permanent partner and then realize that there was nothing more than some laughs but little else. The same thinking goes in this example: when there is a deep, interesting conversation, although maybe it lacks sparks at the beginning, in the long term it could give the person meaningful companionship that might last forever.

When talking about relationships, it's not the right moment to use logic. But you can use logic in terms of understanding how we usually love everything in the short term and how we like to procrastinate. Intuition makes us think that enjoying life is enjoying the now; therefore that sounds short term. No, that's not enjoying the now. Enjoying the now in this case is avoiding the anxiety created by trying to have everything you want now. Gut feeling also tells us that it's bad to procrastinate, that we must be active and finish everything right now. Well, that's not true either. In many circumstances, procrastination is the best option you can choose.

## CHAPTER SIXTEEN

CLICHÉS

What do clichés have to do with all that has been written in this book? If you haven't figured it out yet, this book for the most part goes against common thinking. Common thinking can be categorized as a cliché in certain ways. Maybe these are clichés that are not as frequently used in daily conversations like "think outside the box" or "like taking candy from a baby." Those are so commonly used that every time you hear them, you get pissed. It is disturbing because people love to hear new ideas, new ways of saying things. We don't all want to be the same, saying exactly the same words, the same ideas, and coming to the same conclusions. One of the most interesting things in human contact is learning new perspectives. Clichés in some ways try to make all of us think the same way.

Many clichés are taken as facts, and nobody discusses them. One cliché I think is really a good one (Pitbull even used it in one of his songs) is "The grass is always greener on the other side." It means that people think that others' situations are better than their situation. If we analyze this one, it can be quite real for most people. I don't think Bill Ackman would ever use that cliché. I doubt any of his neighbors are in a better situation than he is. Well, not because we all know Bill Ackman as a rich and smart man, but we don't know him in many other areas of his life that don't have to do with money or intelligence (or style or good looks or Ivy League education, or magna cum laude degree or philanthropic causes etc., etc.). Maybe he is happy; maybe he isn't. The truth is inside him. Even though it might be true in most cases, it isn't a fact, but it seems that nobody questions that bright cliché.

In general, one of the best qualities in humans is their originality. Being faithful to their own essence is one of the main characteristics that makes a person attractive enough to be heard. People not only use clichés but think in a clichéd way. Thinking in a clichéd way denotes that someone lacks creativity and a sense of humor. Many times, good humor comes from the unthinkable. That surprise is an important part of what makes something funny. On the other hand, if a deep conversation is needed or wanted at a specific moment, this is when creativity is the main component. Many people think that knowledge is what's most useful in a deep or interesting conversation. Knowledge can be vast, but if it doesn't have enough creativity and spark, it can probably be extremely boring. Nobody wants to get involved in a conversation that seems like a Second World War TV documentary (black and white edition), lots of knowledge and lots of yawns. It's not that knowledge is not important. It's extremely important but only combined with creativity and focus.

Life is transmitted through literature and dialogue. Mainly by dialogue, because very often only the most important things are printed. If there's a negotiation, a chat with your boss, some public relations talk, an acclaimed speech, entertaining your kids, or getting involved in a romantic conversation, knowledge alone is not going to help you out with an outstanding accomplishment. For that purpose, creativity is the boost everybody needs, and consequently avoiding clichés is the way out.

Some might think that if creativity comes from the right side of the brain, it doesn't make sense that the clichés could be avoided by using logic. Wouldn't it be by intuition? Well, it doesn't work that way. Creativity does involve the right side of the brain. In that part is where creativity starts. But then, you must give form to that new idea, and most of the tools needed to do that are found in the left side of your brain. So for being creative you need the whole brain. There are studies that confirm this.[96]

There are some clichés that are used as a shortcut instead of giving a very long explanation. It is somewhat like jargon, even though jargon is more words than phrases. It's used in a company or within an industry to say very specific things without the need to give extra explanation. It is useful for avoiding misunderstandings. It is definitely more beneficial than harmful.

The constant use of clichés turns your brain lazy, avoiding thinking in new ways to say things, express ideas, or tell stories. It doesn't mean that it should be a confusing way of communicating. The focus is clear communication but with an original way of thinking.

Overrating clichés is quite curious. People don't think they use them, but they do. The problem is that they come in automatic mode. If you ask, people hate clichés, but many times it is the easiest way they can communicate. It's easier to replicate ideas than to create them. That's what a cliché is.

Communication, in the complex way that humans do it, is one of the main abilities that separates us from animals. Animals also communicate among themselves but in a different way. Human communication is more complete. It's important for people to focus on improving their communication for the rest of their lives. It is something that will really improve everything they do. If they know how to do something but are vague communicating it, the impact will be minimal. People should train their brains to always think in an original way, original in creating and communicating. If they only want to use other people's ideas or clichés, it is not going to be enough. Those ideas of others could be used as a base and then added to a lot, not in their communication but in their thinking.

That original way of thinking is something that people should use, an introspection to know what their actual methodology of thinking is. Most people think in a clichéd way. The problem is not just using the clichés. That is only the cause of a clichéd way of thinking. A way to avoid this clichéd thinking is having a lot of information while having the ability to synthesize. Having the power to infer various types of information is critical; if you can't, you won't be able to communicate those ideas. With so much information and knowledge, it's easier to have that power of original thinking. The more info you've got, the more creativity you can gain.

Without knowledge it's difficult for creativity to flow. The main driver is having the will to attain knowledge, then the thinking and communication come from something that is more difficult to have if you weren't born with it. That is curiosity. Without the initial curiosity, the flow of all the processes will get stuck. As mentioned before, the thing you need most to develop all these abilities is time. All these processes take a lot of time.

When you have the ideas, communication is totally the opposite way to the thinking part. In thinking, you need to gain millions of ideas from many people, which will be used to develop your own way of thinking. Communication itself is the other way around: not adding to someone else's communication but subtracting. The ideal in communication is telling complex ideas with the fewest possible words without losing the sense. In other words, communicate difficult things briefly but in a way that everybody can understand (and not get bored).

If someone communicates in an original way, there's a high possibility that the idea will be captured by the audience. The attributes of an idea that will stick in someone's mind should have three things: simplicity, originality, and relevance.

There are some people who memorize quotes from movies. Why is that, besides maybe loving the movie? It's because in the movie, they said that for the first time and in an original way, which makes it "sticky." If someone introduces you to the current US president and he presents himself: "Hi, I'm Trump. Donald Trump." Besides laughing, he doesn't sound like James Bond at all; more than that, he is not James Bond, who is the only one allowed to use that way of introducing himself. So Trump better create his own way of saying hello if he wants to deviate from the norm. In this case, it may be a cliché even though nobody uses it. That phrase is so unique to its creator that anyone who uses it will be considered ridiculous. This extremely well-known phrase is useful to figure out how ridiculous someone is when using it. There are some phrases that are not as famous as that one, but it is always important to remember: if using Bond's phrasing will make you sound ridiculous, using some other lesser known cliché will make you sound just... a little less ridiculous.

Clichés are sometimes useful as shortcuts to avoid over explanation. The problem is entering into a mode in which you communicate in a clichéd way that turns boring and, worse than that, when you start to think in a clichéd way. If that's the case, your ideas will be boring because they lack originality. Originality in thinking and communication is the best way to transmit knowledge. That way you keep people engaged; therefore, the message is clearly understood. The key to having this originality is having a lot of information. That information and analysis is not instinctive. Filling your head with information you can analyze comes from deep dedication, focus, and time. It's hard work; it doesn't come from nowhere.

## CHAPTER SEVENTEEN

CREATING MEMORIES

Memories are created in different ways. We desperately want to save certain types of information on our hard disks, but in many cases it doesn't happen. On the other hand, there are memories that are created from experiences, which usually are easier to remember. Sometimes these are good for our well-being, and sometimes it is better to forget them.

Going deeply into different experiences, let's analyze nostalgia. There are pros and cons to engaging in nostalgia. Nostalgia (not to be mistaken with melancholy) appeared centuries ago, when it was considered a neurological disease. The word has its origins as a sort of homesickness. In 1688 the Swiss doctor Johannes Hofer mentioned it for the first time in a dissertation. Referring to Swiss mercenaries (soldiers on duty helping other countries for pay), he said that when out of their country on missions, they had a feeling of missing home. In contrast, melancholy is considered an illness and is a subtype of clinical depression, which requires treatment. People tend to use *nostalgia* and *melancholy* as synonyms.

Nowadays, nostalgia is not considered a malady, but there's no definitive answer as to whether being nostalgic is good or bad. Studies say that people can benefit from it, and on the other hand, it can make people's lives worse. One study that supports the positive side of nostalgia comes from the University of Southampton, England.[97] Even though memories may not all be positive, the outcome can end up being positive. Summarizing, the positive outcomes of this study mention a feeling of belonging and affirmation, becoming more generous with others, and feeling that we are valuable and have valuable lives. There's just one thing to consider in this study: *avoidance*. It's a psychological term referring to a type of personality that avoids contact with something or someone who creates stress. In general, certain people avoid social contact because they don't feel comfortable and to protect themselves from psychological damage. Therefore, people can be classified as having a low- or high-avoidance personality. Low avoidance refers to people who feel comfortable in social situations, whereas high avoidance is the opposite. Those with low-avoidance personalities are the ones who benefit from nostalgia.

Let's look at meditation. It's a difficult activity as it's not easy to do it the right way due to high expectations. People start to lose focus and interest when they see that it doesn't give them fast results, as people usually like in any activity. Good things in life don't usually give you fast results. Attaining good things takes time.

To conquer meditation, it's a long way to travel. Many people misunderstand meditation. They think that the goal is having a blank mind. First, there's no tangible goal in meditation as there is in other activities. The goal is enlightenment (Nirvana). This is an easy way to describe a goal. *Goal* is a term that is understandable in human terms. Nirvana is something so difficult to explain that language doesn't have the words. The experts say it takes years just to understand the concept. It's not possible to explain it using the mind. If it can be called a goal, it's something almost impossible for most people to attain. An intermediate goal might be enjoying the moment, improving focus, developing awareness, decluttering your mind of useless repeated thoughts, or gaining patience, among others.

Mantras are ancient phrases that, through repetition, help you keep focus and avoid having a lot of different thoughts every second. There are several alternatives to mantras, such as breathing; focusing on how your breath goes in and out helps you dissipate that avalanche of thoughts. Another is focusing step by step and relaxing each part of your body, putting a lot of focus on each part. There are others, but these are the most common.

When you are using one of these techniques to meditate successfully, your brain starts to create blank spaces. Take the mantra technique, for example. You start to repeat the mantra several times, and while you're repeating it, there are a lot of thoughts going through your mind. At that moment you are doing out two things at the same time: mentally repeating the mantra and holding different thoughts. After a while, your brain starts to think about anything for a little moment. In that time, you don't think of the mantra or any thought. This is the blank mind. It usually lasts a few seconds at most. If you continue, these blank spaces start to appear increasingly, not just more frequently, but for a longer period each time. This process is not the same for everyone. Some might achieve this quickly; for others it might take a lot longer. It's a totally personal process.

Consequently, the goal of meditation is not having a blank mind; rather it is having focus and relaxation while stretching those blank spaces.

Let's compare meditation to a film. A film consists of around one hundred and fifty thousand frames. These film frames are photos. In this example, imagine that you think in film frames. They start to pass through your mind (in a movie, they pass at forty-four frames per second), and suddenly, after thirty seconds, two frames are blank. Then thirty seconds more pass, and five frames are blank. Twenty seconds later, five frames are blank. The point of this simile is that, when you are meditating, imagine that your thoughts come in images or just units of ideas. First, you don't have to hang on to any of the thoughts that appear; you must let them pass through. As the film frames pass through your mind, you suddenly start to see the blank frames. The objective here is to increase the number and length of the blank film segments. The goal isn't to have, for example, thirty minutes of blank space. It's just stretching the spaces without trying to reach a specific frequency. Meditation is not a competition with anybody. It's exactly the opposite. It's reaching enlightenment (if you can), which is the end of suffering. It's reaching it but without trying too hard.

Memories are an essential part of the human experience. Let's focus on memories as part of entertainment, not those memories that you need to be functional in your daily life. If you have constant problems recalling important information, you'll have problems at work and in everyday activities. If this happens, it might be a pathology, and for this there may be no cure.

Memories as something we consciously or unconsciously use in a psychological way are a different thing. Usually most people love to create and have good memories. People like to collect them. The purpose can be pure satisfaction or to use them as raw material for telling stories.

Even though in theory, some western studies may say that, as a minimum, nostalgic positive effects beat the negative ones, according to ancient Eastern philosophy it is possible to deduct different outcomes of nostalgia.

Nostalgic thoughts should be those blank frames in the comparison of meditation to film but in the opposite way. Instead of increasing the frequency and length of those blank frames, the goal with these nostalgic thoughts should be their decrease. The blank frames in this case just bring you attachment to feelings. Attachment to the past. It doesn't matter if they are positive or negative feelings. It's easy to get attached to both.

According to ancient Eastern philosophy, getting rid of attachments will make your life more enjoyable. Attachment to things only places you in search of more things. To clarify a misconception about attachment, it is not only about physical things as some might think. It also refers to thoughts, to ideas, to everything that's repetitive or obsessive in our minds. This isn't easy to liberate yourself from. If you live in the past, you are principally living in a nostalgic mood, and if you are living in the future, you are generating anxiety and more stress in your life than is needed. The present moment is the only one that allows you to fully enjoy life.

So why are people constantly trying to create new experiences to have good memories about them when it's better to reduce the prioritization of those memories and try to live and enjoy the present moment? These memories should be created as a by-product, which means they are secondary. The main part is the experience in the present.

People are attached to creating memories even if they don't have the rational possibility of doing so. For example, taking expensive trips so they and their kids remember them for the rest of their lives. Few would say, "We want to go to really enjoy that place." People want to increase their archive of memories combined with photographs that help them remember in case their memories fail. It sounds a little overrated in a sense that everyone should fill their lives with memories, creating memories in order to have a fulfilled life.

The older people get, the more nostalgic they become. According to a study, the levels of nostalgia tend to be high in young adults then dip in middle age and rise again during old age.[98]

That is a fact, but it's not the way it should be. In many cases it is old people comparing themselves to their young selves, what they used to do, or what young people are currently doing or spending their time on. They victimize themselves, thinking or saying that they can't do many things now, so they mainly live with and for their memories. That shouldn't be the thinking. There are activities of leisure, work, and learning for every age. Instead of living memories, start learning something feasible for your age. Why not learn to play backgammon or golf? Do puzzles, take a walk in the park, go to the movies, read, investigate something, or write. There are millions of activities more useful for your mood than sitting down and just remembering those good old times.

Who says that good times are only for the young? Isn't Warren Buffett at eighty-eight years old, enjoying life by reading for 80 percent of his working day, investing for 20 percent, and then playing bridge in his free time (and playing some ukulele)? Why not, instead of remembering moments, just continue creating them? If you are such a fan of your memories because your life has been so great, it would be better to write a biography. If it wasn't that interesting or full of amazing achievements, why don't do something so you live a life that's worth reading about in a biography? Even if you don't achieve it, the process will surely be more entertaining and fulfilling than ruminating on nostalgic thoughts.

How about the memories we do want to remember? Even if we want to focus on them, it turns out that is very difficult to do, and it becomes more difficult as we age. There are many tricks and exercises designed to improve your memory: doing math exercises, completing puzzles and crosswords, learning a new language, doing aerobic exercises, and playing chess or card games. The point of this analysis is not to talk about which exercises are better or worse. The point is to decide whether or not we should invest time in creating memories to save in our brains.

In contrast to negative memories created by experiences, that we want to forget, there is some information we want to preserve in our brains. Wouldn't it be great if we remembered everything we learned in our teenage years in world history class? The problem is that we may remember some very general information, but most names and dates and lots of details are totally lost, at least by our conscious memory. Worse than that, it is not just information that we learned maybe decades ago. How about trying to recall information you learned from a book you read a month ago and finding that most of the details have already disappeared?

The same is true with a plot of a novel. Try to recall the names of the characters in a John Grisham novel. It turns out to be even more difficult if you have read several of his books. You start to forget or confuse which character was in which one. It's even more difficult because there are some characters that appear in more than one of his novels. You end up mixing up characters and just remembering the main story. You start losing the details over time, and after a while, even the plot will be difficult to recall.

This doesn't only happen with written material, of course. It's exactly the same with movies or the TV news. Try to remember the details of a movie that it's not favorite. (You might remember the details of your favorite movie). It's very difficult. Many times, a reminder is needed to conjure up some details of the movie. Not only by someone asking you if you remember one specific part of the movie. If you watch the movie again, you might know what's coming.

The forgetting curve is a curse we all must deal with. The concept first appears in 1885 in the work of German psychologist Hermann Ebbinghaus. The point is that, depending on the importance of the topic or the impression it made on you, newly learned information starts fading abruptly. After twenty minutes, you retain only 58 percent of what you have learned. After twenty-four hours, retention is only 33 percent. It continues decreasing, and after thirty-one days, the retention is around 21 percent.[99] (This does not apply or applies less to specific important moments of life, such as when you watch a movie that turns out to be your favorite. Or a shocking moment like the conclusion of a divorce settlement. These types of things might stay crystal clear in your mind for many years.)

It is obvious that most people don't know how this concept works, but from experience they know that it is not easy to remember things. Even though they don't know that after one day, 67 percent of a memory is lost, they know they can't remember most new info.

Why is it that even though people know they are going to forget anything new—for example, a book—they continue reading? Or go to a movie when after a month 79 percent of the information will have vanished? Worse than that, they watch the nightly news, but when they wake up in the morning, they only know 36 percent[3] of what they watched last night. Why do people still do it?

Maybe people still do all these "soon-to-vanish" activities because their subconscious minds have the need to enjoy the moment. People might not be aware that they should do it but we might be programmed for this. In a very deep part of ourselves, there is something that tells us that the right thing to do is to enjoy that specific moment.

Have you ever forgotten about a concert you went to several years ago? Or even worse, tried to remember all the songs that were performed there the next day? It's impossible. In time, the only thing you are left with from that concert is the feeling that you had a great moment, nothing more. You won't even remember who you went to the concert with!

So, to summarize, there are two types of memories we are analyzing here. Let's call them Type I and Type II.

Type I memories and experiences are the ones we want to create as much as possible, believing that remembering them when we get old will make our lives more fulfilled.

---

[3] On Hermann Ebbinghaus's self-measured forgetting curve, after nine hours, retention is 36 percent.

Type II memories are the knowledge we need to remember, so it can be used for different purposes. They can be practical or just for the pleasure of expanding our knowledge.

People are desperate to create Type I and Type II memories and remember them. It doesn't matter if they are experiences or knowledge. They believe that both will enrich their lives in terms of pleasure and happiness. The curious part is that with the Type I, those are experiences as memories that aren't worth creating. It's OK to create them, but it shouldn't be the goal. This is because many times people do things they end up not liking, or others where is not smart to spend time and money, just to create experiences. Maybe it is a new experience that people think that first you need to try it to discover if you like it or not. This may apply to some types of experiences, but for most of them, there is something inside that tells you whether you are going to like the new experience or not. You don't need to compete in Mixed Martial Arts (MMA) to know if it's something you like. Without trying it, you know if it's your type of hobby or not. The goal should be enjoying the moment since that is the thing that will make you happier. The memory created is just a by-product of the experience, which will fade more and more over time. Consequently, the important part is the moment, not the memory.

On the other hand, we need Type II memories to retain knowledge, which is almost impossible to do. With Type II memories, it is as important, if not more so, to enjoy the moment focusing on the knowledge. Even though it will fade in time, there are techniques that help you retain the knowledge and improve the forgetting curve. For example, rereading a book has been proven to make that knowledge stick. Or talking about what you learned with someone. It can be in a casual conversation or in a book club. What makes things stick in your brain has a lot to do with repetition. So even though you must enjoy something you want to learn; focus, work, time, and repetition are important with Type II memories. Well, perhaps it's not necessary to enjoy something you need to learn. If you want to get a driver's license, you might not enjoy studying for the written test, but you must study for it even if you don't like it. As with the Type I memories, your subconscious mind is telling you that the important part is to enjoy moments.

Intuition might tell us that to be happy in life, we must create memories. Some people say, "That's why I work—to enjoy my free time with all the effort I put into earning that money," mainly enjoying, in this case, by buying things and making those experiences that transforms into memories. Logic tells us that memory fades too easily, and maybe there are other options besides what feels the most obvious to be happy in life. Both Type I and Type II memories will fade in time, and only a small part of them will be left. The only thing that keeps you tuned in to happiness is to go with that flow—the flow of creating knowledge and experiences just for the sake of enjoying them.

## CHAPTER EIGHTEEN

OPTIMIZING TIME

We all as human beings are taught from the beginning of our lives that we must make everything fast in an optimal way. We should meet deadlines; if not, life is going to be tough on us. From elementary school through college, master's degree or PhD, we are measured with numbers that tell us how we are doing. We could be doing great, regular or "why don't you better do a different thing?" Being good or great at each stage will help you succeed in life. It's not guaranteed, but it will drastically increase your chances of success. Success, as defined in the capitalist world, means a lot of money or at least financial freedom. That's supposed to bring all of us what we need for a happy life.

In some sense it's true; you need money to be happy—not millions but, according to studies you need at least $75,000 a year to optimize happiness in terms of financial necessities. Having more is not going to hurt, but it isn't going to make much difference to your happiness.

We are trained to do everything in an optimal way. We are told since childhood that, to go from point A to point B, humans naturally choose the shortest and fastest route. If we must choose one of two equal products, we will choose the cheaper one. It's quite absurd not to take the fastest route; life should always be optimized. That's what smart people do. That's the message.

Why should we take the shortest route to go from point A to point B? That decision might be natural in human nature, but that doesn't mean it is the smartest choice. Would you do that if you were told that the longest route involved Bono chatting with fans giving free backstage passes to his concert? If the longest route were much safer while the shortest had a high crime rate? What if the longest route had an incredible panoramic view, or you just wanted to walk and have a little more time to stretch your legs? There are mountain climbers who choose the longest route to summit a mountain on purpose. Why? Just for fun.

This view of the shortest route possible is not literal. It also means as fast as possible. Do we really need to do everything as fast as possible? Yes, in a line at bank, waiting for an elevator, or waiting for an elevator to close its doors, we'd like astonishing speed, but if you're test-driving a Ferrari, would you want it to be fast? Yes, you would like to go fast in it; I don't mean that. I mean would you want five minutes to test-drive or a complete drive along the Grande Corniche in France? I hope the second one. How about sex? Thirty seconds isn't something to be proud of; much more than that would be better.

We as humans are biologically programmed to take the easiest way to do something if the expected results are the same. We are naturally going to optimize the process, not just traveling from A to B but with any project that requires a route to be completed and is allotted a certain amount of time. The point is that great discoveries usually take place when the unexpected appears while you were waiting for the expected. There is a much greater possibility that, by taking the easiest path, you'll discover only what you expect, not what you don't. Many times what you don't expect is much bigger and impactful than the initial trial. The reason is that the longest and most complicated routes contain many more variables; that's why they're longer and more challenging. The more variables you have, the greater the possibility of avoiding being blind to new options. One of the greatest minds in history, Leonardo da Vinci, dominated this art of not taking the easiest or fastest path. One of his works, the *Mona Lisa*, considered one of the most important masterpieces in history and the most valuable painting in the world, was painted with such patience that it took Leonardo sixteen years to finish it.[100]

The point is that we really have a very short time to do many important things in life while for others we really need to take time and not necessarily choose the fastest and easiest way. It's confusing and not obvious which ones should be done fast and why and which ones we should take our time doing.

Some decisions are life changing. Where you were born, the family you were born into, where you go to school, what type of job you select, and how good you are at it while in your twenties practically define your future for the next sixty years.

The most important factor for success in the capitalist world is the country and family you were born in. Neither was possible for you to decide, but they could have been planned by your parents.

Where you were born is something your parents could have decided if they had planned matters carefully. They could have modified their lives in such a way as to have their children in a country with greater possibilities for success. There are countries that grant nationality according to blood heritage, as for example in Switzerland and Austria, so those wouldn't be good options, but there are others like the United States that confer citizenship on everyone born on American soil.

Another option would have been to live in a country for a period of five to ten years; in this way almost any nationality on earth is guaranteed. There are a lot of people who have successfully done it. Undoubtedly your future is much brighter (even though it's not guaranteed) if you have an American rather that a Ghanaian passport.

What family you were born into may seem like something that neither you nor your parents could have decided. The reality is that your parents had the chance to decide. If a couple is not in a position to raise kids without grave difficulties, it's totally in their hands to decide whether to have kids or not. Nobody forces them. It's their responsibility to determine if they are able to raise successful kids. Nothing will guarantee raising successful kids, but there are several things that increase their chances. The obvious one is their own equity or expectations of future earnings. Even if many people don't want to admit it, relying only on love will not turn them into successful kids; sadly they cost a lot, so you'll need a lot of money. Money is not the only thing, but without it, it may be impossible.

These two things are extremely important, but there are other important aspects to raising a child. Beyond money, each person should analyze and decide if they are capable and have the patience, time, love, intelligence, and passion to raise a child. If they don't have these five things, how will they succeed? Is there any other activity in life in which you can succeed without patience, passion, love, intelligence, and time? I don't think so; that's why they're requirements for success.

These five things are not related to money, but money helps to invest in things that you as a parent can then give a child. Formal education and learning in general require an outlay by parents. That's why money is important when raising them.

The final thing a parent can do in terms of making a smart decision on whether to have children or not is predicting if their genes transmission is adequate as a tool for a kid's success. If everything is normal, it's difficult to estimate that, but there may be some warnings about illnesses that parents are better off deciding whether or not to transmit to their kids. It's totally up to them, but they should be very clear that it's a variable that's only in their hands.

This may sound coldhearted, but think about when someone is infertile and decides to buy sperm or adopt. What do they search for: any sperm or any child for adoption? Not at all. Why, when people have their own child, don't they care about their genetic problems? These include depression, schizophrenia, heart problems, diabetes, Parkinson's disease, and Alzheimer's, among others. They also don't care about possible problems generated by their way of living, such as drug and alcohol abuse or STDs, for example.

Why are they so keen when they are looking for another man's sperm but don't take the time or care about to analyze their own? They leave that part to luck. When they purchase sperm, they search for a donor who is at least five feet eight inches tall (there are sperm banks that don't accept sperm from donors shorter than five feet eight)[101] with a high preference for those six feet or taller. Have you ever heard a man saying he's not having kids because he's only five feet six inches tall? They tend to underestimate their own qualities, but they are very strict with those of others.

Take Brazil as an example. This is one of the fastest-growing markets in sperm imports. The preference in terms of physical qualities of the donor (what kind of sperm users are buying), 95.4 percent comes from donors of white ancestry, 51.8 percent are blue eyed, and 90.7 percent have brown or blond hair.[102] These are the preferences. This doesn't only apply to Brazil. The clear majority of the sperm stock of the Seattle Sperm Bank is from blond-haired, blue-eyed Caucasian donors.[103] People here are not buying just any sperm. They are buying what they consider better sperm, so the sperm bank provides what people demand. They prefer that their child has a higher probability of being tall, white with blue eyes and light-colored hair. That's it. They think that those physical qualities will help give their children a better future.

Fairfax Cryobank, a very well-known sperm bank, proudly declares that it has the highest-quality donor sperm, saying that only 1 percent of applicants are accepted as donors.[104] If we translated this strict process to the general population, how many would qualify to be fathers under the same standards?

If a renowned sperm bank is doing this type of screening, it's because they have clients who want to buy what they are selling. This way, their clients can buy only the best. On the other hand, when people are thinking about their own qualities for procreation, they don't care if they have the best or not; they just care about leaving a legacy in this world.

Those two things—where you were born and whether or not you should have been born—were decisions of your parents, and often they would have decided very fast. These two things also apply to you when deciding to have your own family—not for your future but for your kids' future, if you decide to have them.

You should decide as quickly as possible if the place you're living is adequate to give birth to a child and, if it isn't, move to a better place. The same applies for predicting your general situation. You should know with some accuracy if you are going to be able to take care of a child financially for the next eighteen to twenty-two years—not just raising the child but also giving them the tools they need to improve their chances of a successful life. If your prediction doesn't show a high probability of reaching this goal, avoiding that project sounds like a smarter choice. You shouldn't wait until the day the pill doesn't work or maybe confuse which days are safe to have sex.

You also shouldn't assume that the developing country you are living in, is going to be a rich country in a few years or decades, so your future offspring will have a lot of opportunities. Bad idea because it's almost certainly not going to happen. Don't expect that your kid, even though they will come into this world in poor conditions, in a poor country, and with zero equity, might be an outlier and thus go to Stanford on a full scholarship. They're not likely to accomplish that either.

There is a third thing that is not something parents can decide but is the decision of each person. This also should be decided fast. It's about what to study and where to start your first job or entrepreneurial project. This shouldn't be as difficult as it seems. Most people are not happy in their jobs mainly because they didn't study for a career they love. Why not? Usually because they don't love anything and don't feel that they are extremely good at or have a special talent for anything. Many would say in their forties, "I should have studied architecture." The problem is that is a little too late.

Twenty-two years too late to be precise. It's not easy to afford going back college and then start an entry-level job when you are raising a family for example. The problem is that when you discover what you really like, it's usually too late. So, how can someone decide fast early on if most don't have a clear passion for anything in their youth?

The key is not selecting something you love. Just select something that can give you a good financial future that you are somewhat attracted to—not necessarily love but are OK with. One thing that every eighteen-year-old should understand is that the teachings of a study program at college are very different from what they will end up doing at their job. In college, you will learn a lot of things that you might be using in a company maybe after fifteen years, first doing some work that has little to do with what you've learned. During that period, you might be disappointed and decide you don't like that profession. Maybe it's because you haven't reached a position where things start to turn interesting. You might also reach a point at which you use the information you learned in college, but even though you use it, you still don't like it.

This sounds like the opposite of what you usually hear; as the cliché goes, "Find something you love, and you'll never have to work a day in your life." The point is that, like most people, if you don't love something, it's better to find something that can let you enjoy life in general and reach financial freedom someday. The usual recommendation is, "You spent half your life at the office, so you'd better do something you like." Well, not so fast. Let's look at the numbers.

Depending on the country, vacations and official holidays vary, but here's a general approach:

B		Days/year	365
C		Weekends	104
D		Vacations	20
E		Holidays	10
F	=B-C-D-E	#Working days	231
H	=Fx8	#Working hours	1,848

Deducting weekends, vacations, and holidays, on average, people work 231 days a year.

That's a total of 1,848 hours a year.

Now, let's consider a person who works thirty-five years in total, from ages twenty-five to sixty. (This is an approximation since people generally take some time off for different reasons, like a layoff, additional studies, a sabbatical, illness, or just wanting some time to rest.) In that period:

A		# Years	35
F	=B-C-D-E	#Working days	231
H	=Fx8	#Working hours	1,848
J	=HxA	#Working hours	64,680

A person will work on average 64,680 hours.

Now let's see how many hours a person *doesn't* work in that same thirty-five-year period:

A		# Years	35
B		Days/year	365
F	=B-C-D-E	#Working days	231
G	=B-F	# Nonworking days	134
I	=(Gx24)+(Fx16)	#Nonworking hours	6,912
K	=IxA	#Nonworking hours	241,920

In those thirty-five years, there are a total of 241,920 nonworking hours. This includes the twenty-four hours of the weekends, vacations, and holidays and the daily sixteen free hours during the work weeks, in which people only dedicate eight hours a day to work.

Now let's see the chart of the free hours you'll have from age sixty until age seventy-nine, the age that, on average, people die in OECD countries:[105] (See Appendix L).

A		# Years	19
G	=B-F	# Nonworking days	365
I	=Gx24	#Nonworking hours	8,760
K	=IxA	#Nonworking hours	166,440

These are the final numbers: those free hours while you're working plus the hours of your retirement. (Just a reminder, this is from age twenty-five until age seventy-nine.)

Total working hours	64,680	14%
Total nonworking hours	408,360	86%
Total Hours	473,040	

Let's look at the complete chart:

Working period (25 to 60 years old)

	PERIOD	FORMULA		
A			# Years	35
B			Days/year	365
C			Weekends	104
D			Vacations	20
E			Holidays	10
F		=B-C-D-E	#Working days	231
G	a Year	=B-F	# Nonworking days	134
H		=Fx8	#Working hours	1,848
I		=(Gx24)+(Fx16)	#Nonworking hours	6,912
J	Working Years	=HxA	#Working hours	64,680
K		=IxA	#Nonworking hours	241,920

Nonworking period (60 to 79 years old)

	PERIOD	FORMULA		
A			# Years	19
B			Days/year	365
C			Weekends	
D			Vacations	
E			Holidays	
F		=B-C-D-E	#Working days	
G	a Year	=B-F	# Nonworking days	365
H		=Fx8	#Working hours	
I		=Gx24	#Nonworking hours	8,760
J	Working Years	=HxA	#Working hours	-
K		=IxA	#Nonworking hours	166,440

Total working hours	64,680	14%

Total nonworking hours	408,360	86%

This means that the expression "You spend half your life at the office" really means "You spend 14 percent of your life at the office." (That doesn't include ages zero through twenty-five, when that you aren't at the office either; for the purpose of this analysis, we are counting just from the time you start working.)

The number of hours per year that people work (1,848) is quite close to the 1,759 hours per year that the OECD countries averaged in 2017.[106] (See Appendix M). The number is about the same, 13% of the time working.

How about those lucky countries where work-life balance is amazing, like Germany? Well, they only work 1,356 hours per year. That means that if you tell a German, "You must decide what you love to do because you're going to spend half your life at the office," the German might correct you and say, "Sorry, not half my life, just ten percent."

The OECD country that works the most hours a year is Mexico: 2,257 hours per year. In that case, the percentage of life spent working is 17 percent. In case you're curious, for the United States the number is 13 percent. (See Appendix N).

Some may say, "But you are counting the hours that you're sleeping. That shouldn't count." Why not? If you decide to take a nap, that time doesn't count? It counts as if you were dead? Sleeping is one of the greatest pleasures in life, and sure, it should be counted. Everyone decides how much they want to sleep. If you want to be awake more hours without feeling dizzy from sleep deprivation, you can use the Uberman sleep method in which you sleep just two hours a day without sacrificing anything, supposedly without side effects. Google it. So if you want some six additional hours a day to do whatever you want, there it is; you can have them. It might not work for everyone, but you can give it a try.

Spending 14 percent of your time at something you're not passionate about doesn't sound that bad. It's like dedicating half hour a day to cleaning up your home. Most wouldn't be passionate about doing it, but it's just 2 percent of your daily time; you'll survive that.

So how should careers be selected? Not by looking for the best-paying jobs and then deciding to study that. Some affinity for the career is necessary. The amount of money a job pays should not be seen in absolute terms but in relative terms. One should determine what type of life one wants to have and crunch the numbers to see how much it costs. If the average wage of an attractive career matches that number, go on; that is your choice to dedicate 14 percent of your life to after graduation.

This is a good way to reduce some of the frustration in your life. Frustration comes from not meeting expectations. It's not absolute; it's relative. If your expectations are exceeded, you are happy and fulfilled. If you come up short of your expectations, you might be unsatisfied and frustrated with what you've done. Keep in mind that this only applies if you don't love something special in life. Maybe you love doing something that doesn't pay the amount of money you need for the type of life you want to have. In that case, maybe the fact that you love what you're doing so much compensates in a way for sacrificing that way of life, so it doesn't affect you much.

When you don't love doing anything in particular, you can only rely on the type of life you want to have. That is assuming that your salary is in what could be called the "OK range," and the job is not a total pain. This mainly refers to earning the amount that covers the type of life you want but also certain characteristics in your life that make you match those expectations besides money. Let's look at some examples:

In terms of just matching money to a certain type of life, you can't decide to be a professional barista if you want to live in Palm Beach and send your kids to private schools. The barista salary (that's around $25,000 per year on average) will never match that type of life. For that type of life, you'll need to go for the highest-paid professions—let's say, in the field of law or finance. Not even those professions will guarantee that life, but you might get closer. On the other hand, if your expectations are to live in a developing country, in a small house in a not-fancy place, and be childless, maybe being a barista will match that type of life perfectly, and you might be nothing but fulfilled.

It ends up being more important to match that income and the type of life rather than the love of the job by itself. At the end, 86 percent of the time is a great amount of time in your life to enjoy what has been paid with the income of that not-so-loved job.

There are other variables besides money in the selection of a career. These are the characteristics of your life and the context in which you want to develop it. Would you like to be an airline pilot, not necessarily because you like piloting the plane but because you're attracted to the type of life a pilot has? Sleeping in hotels fifteen days a month with free meals and traveling around many different cities makes you more excited that being behind a desk eight hours a day. Others might choose a profession that has to do with the ocean, such as being a marine biologist. This might be because they love animals and life at the beach, so they can complement their job with sixteen free, lazy hours every day at their beachside house. This type of life might compensate for the discomfort of the profession; at least you can have the type of life you want.

There is the best-of-both-worlds strategy. That is loving some career that happens to pay for the lifestyle you like while having a special talent for it. Great if you are that kind of person. But keep in mind that if you're not in that position, there's a second-best option.

It's curious that the decisions you are supposed to take time making are often much better when made as soon as possible. If that is the case and those three things are analyzed (where you were born, in which family, and choosing your career) should then be decided on fast. Which are the ones that should be decided slowly? Well, basically most of the rest. Unless you work in an emergency room, as a soldier in war, as an air traffic controller, or in those types of professions in which each second passes really counts, most things in life are better when you take your time doing them. The probability of error really increases when things are done fast. It's almost always better to do things without errors, with deep analysis, and with logic more than with intuition than to do them really fast.

Most things in life aren't needed as fast as possible. People who do things without (or with the fewest) errors because they take the time needed are really exceptional and are the ones who are going to excel in life. An individual error is not usually penalized. What is penalized is the sum of errors, which is mostly due to lack of focus and not dedicating the amount of time that each activity requires. The sum of errors is what makes people fail, falling short in their goals. So, assuming you are already born because your parents decided wisely whether or not they should have you, then choosing an OK profession fast, sticking with it, and while there do things slowly for high achievement is a great combination for success.

## CHAPTER NINETEEN

"INTUITIVELESS"

In life we must deal with problems every day from the moment we are born. When we are babies, we have to get attention when we want food. At that time, that is the main problem. Then throughout life, problems keep increasing, and even when we get old and retire, we continue dealing with problems. Even if we decide to stay home, problems keep coming. Bills that we should keep paying until our last day, health issues, being bored and not knowing how to remedy that, not having done what supposedly would have made us happy in life, regretting things that we should have done differently or things that we never gave a try... Every problem can be solved but with different approaches. We basically come to earth to solve problems. Solving problems is what makes us grow. The greater the quantity and difficulty of problems we solve, the better we'll get through life.

How is it that any problem can be solved? It doesn't sound convincing. We deal with problems basically with two different approaches: with a rational and logical focus or with a more common-sense intuitive focus.

There are easy and practical problems that many times can be solved with intuition. If you want to decorate your room, a little intuition and getting some ideas from specialized magazines might be enough to do a pretty good job. You don't need to study the theory of colors deeply to create something nice. It's different if you are talking about being an interior designer. In that case, you should definitely study and know the many concepts of the profession.

There are also very important problems to be solved for which the intuitive approach is still the optimal one. How about love? Love is something that can't be measured. If you've been with someone for a while, you might start thinking that maybe it is time to take the next step. Is it time to get married? Logic is not going to be as useful as intuition. Through intuition you know if you are with the right person. You know how much you love that person and how much that person loves you. Love is not logical; it is a feeling that must be dealt with through intuition, not with logic. There can be situations in which, for example, you might be in love with a criminal, and it doesn't seem logical to be with that person. In that case, your intuition should have analyzed that that's not the correct path to follow in the first place.

The same happens with existential problems. These are the types of problems that are considered impossible to solve, but, yes, they can be solved. Not in the sense of knowing an answer, but for example, suppose you want to be from a different race than your own. You can't change it; that's clear. But a way to solve the problem might be through a spiritual approach, through meditation, or by several other methods or ways of thinking that make you deeply accept who you are. That has nothing to do with logic. What's your mission in life, and why did you come to earth in this life? No logical approach will answer that question completely either.

If we could divide this book into main topics, there are three. These topics were selected because of their importance in life: human relations, optimizing money, and refining decisions. They weren't grouped that way in the book on purpose. To avoid having it look like a "recipe" book, saying "This is the way life should be lived," or "The decisions in this book are the ones everybody should make for their lives." As stated in the introduction, this book is about ideas on how to react in the moment we should make a decision. Many ideas seem practical and can be applied to someone's personal life if he or she consider. But the main purpose behind all these ideas is to promote a way of thinking that can be applied to many different problems we all must face. In general terms, the topics selected were those that at first glance a solution to it might be ideal by an intuitive approach but thinking through it was demonstrated that using rational thinking is a better idea. By mistake, lately that rational thinking has been seconded by gut feelings that many times are totally overrated.

Besides those important problems previously mentioned for which an intuitive approach is ideal, there are others that are critical in life such as, "Why have children when you can't take care of those costs?" We discovered that something that costs around a thousand dollars a month, might seem cheap. By examining the numbers and researching some data, we figured out that one child costs the same as the median net worth per capita of the richest country in the world (Switzerland). What seems cheap, ends up not being as it looked at first glance. Never underestimate the power of compound interest! Going deeper into this same point could raise the question "Why not have children when it's the most important experience of a human being in terms of happiness?" Using facts, we also discovered that in 64 percent of the OECD countries researched, childless people were happier than parents. And how about that scary feeling of being lonely or sad once you get old if you decide not to have children? Not a problem— most childless old people (men and women) don't feel sadder or lonelier than their counterparts who had children. Last thing to highlight: it's the only decision in life you can't regret; there's no way back.

Why choose the perfect career when you've been searching for years to discover something you love, and you still can't find it? Maybe the answer here is to stop searching for something you love and select something that's in the OK range and can give you the type of life you want. In the end, you will only dedicate 14 percent of your time to it.

One of the most important topics in this book is the importance of living in the moment. As humans we were created with a limited memory; it vanishes easily. Much rational data can drive us to the conclusion that the purpose of that design might be to force us to focus on enjoying the moment rather than on creating memories that will later be used for nostalgia. If we are designed to forget most things, the only thing that lasts is enjoying everything while it happens.

The term *intuitiveless* doesn't exist. This word means to avoid living a clichéd life. It means not letting intuition guide every aspect of your life because you might get the wrong outcome. Life has tried to standardize intuition. Try to separate intuition from beliefs and common sense. Those three are not the same.

There are ways of making decisions that should be transmitted by each generation, but they are mostly useful for the not-so-important things. For the most important things in life, those recommendations that try to homogenize every human generally don't make sense. It seems that what we've learned since we were kids is what we call intuition today. Do you want children because your intuition tells you you do, or because your mother told you that it was the right choice in life for you and everyone? That might have been said by your mother so many times that when the time comes, you might feel that you want to have a child through intuition. That's not intuition. It's something somebody taught you.

Nowadays, it's very trendy to follow your gut feelings. It seems the logical part of the brain is underrated and now the important part is the intuitive part. Both sides are great complements: one side starts the creation process, and the other part helps give form to the creation. So during the whole process, whether it's the process of creation or the process of making decisions, you still use both parts. The problem is that if we just follow intuition, we avoid using logic. The objective data that each time is more demonized due to the importance of the spiritual life that each time is held to be more present. Both are important, but we should never leave aside logic, which helps us deal with many issues. The logical part of the brain many times causes us to make the right decisions. It's important to take the time to analyze most of the things that impact our lives. For the most important things, being intuitiveless is the real instinct people should have. It is not the only one, but by thinking deeply while letting our logic flow, we might make the opposite decisions from the ones we assumed we'd make at first glance. Why be intuitive when there is a lot of information that someone has already worked on, and it's usually available for us to make the best decisions? Why be intuitive when we have a complete brain that can be used to its full potential?

There is usually confusion among intuition, instinct and logic. People tend to think that intuition is something that is inside them, and they don't have to make any effort because they were born with it, and it is something that's going to guide them through the many obstacles and decisions to be made in life. That is definitely not the case. That is instinct and we all come to life with it. It's not going to help us with all the obstacles in life but with some. There is a certain type of instinct that is in every human being. For instance, if you see an alligator coming toward you, you know instinctively that you should run. Your body gets fired up with adrenaline, and you become faster and stronger than you've ever been in your life. There is a different kind, similar to instinct but it's intuition. We don't come to the world with it. It comes with the experience and knowledge that you've been accumulating throughout your life. For example, there might be some behaviors and decisions that come intuitively to a professional negotiator. But that intuition come to the professional negotiator because negotiation is a task that involves a lot of theory, logic, and strategy. They only come after years of study and practicing negotiations that make their brains so fast that some things might come as intuition, but only to a very well-trained mind. So, logic and knowledge are the way to get your intuition sharp.

Does being intuitive sometimes mean being lazy? Does intuition replace hard work? Is intuition an excuse for not dedicating time to developing ideas, theories, and best options?

Does intuition mean not using statistical data to support our own theories? Is being intuitive the reason we avoid analyzing the pros and cons of different ideas? Is it the reason we don't think it's necessary to do research? Is it an excuse when we don't have the answer to something?

Is it better to trust your gut or just think?

APPENDIX

APPENDIX A

Where Do Fortune 500 CEOs (Top 100 by Market Capitalization) Live?

Do They Live in Their Hometowns?

Fortune 500
As of March 29, 2018
By market cap

#	Company	CEO	Hometown	Lives	Yes/No	%
1	Apple	Tim Cook	AL	Cupertino, CA	No	
2	Alphabet	Larry Page	MI	Mountain View, CA	No	
3	Microsoft	Satya Nadella	Hyderabad, India	Seattle, WA	No	
4	Amazon	Jeff Bezos	NM	Seattle, WA	No	
5	Berkshire Hathaway	Warren Buffett	Omaha, NE	Omaha, NE	Yes	
6	Facebook	Mark Zuckerberg	NY	Menlo Park, CA	No	
7	JP Morgan Chase	James Dimon	NY	New York, NY	Yes	
8	J&J	Alex Gorsky	KS	NJ	No	
9	ExxonMobil	Darren W. Woods	Irving, TX	KS	No	
10	Bank of America	Brian Moynihan	OH	Charlotte, NC	No	
11	Visa	Alfred F. Kelly Jr.	Creston, NY	San Francisco, CA	No	
12	Walmart	Doug McMillon	AR	Memphis, TN	No	
13	Wells Fargo	Timothy J. Sloan	Cleveland, OH	San Francisco, CA	No	
14	Intel	Brian M. Krzanich	Sta Clara, CA	Sta Clara, CA	Yes	
15	AT&T	Randall Stephenson	Dallas, TX	OK	No	
16	Chevron	Michael K. Wirth	Golden, CO	San RamoN, CA	No	
17	Pfizer	Ian C. Read	Forfar, Scotland	New York, NY	No	
18	United Health Group	David Wichmann	*Not available*	MN		
19	Cisco Systems	Charles H. Robbins	NC	San Jose, CA	No	
20	Home Depot	Craig A. Menear	MI	Atlanta, GA	No	
21	P&G	David S. Taylor	NC	Cincinnati, OH	No	
22	Verizon	Lowell C. McAdam	Buffalo, NY	New York, NY	No	
23	Boeing	Dennis A. Mullenburg	IA	Seattle, WA	No	
24	Oracle	Safra A. Catz/Mark V. Hurd	Israel & New York, NY	Redwood City, CA	No	
25	Coca-Cola	James R. Quincey	UK	Atlanta, GA	No	
26	Mastercard	Ajay Banga	India	New York, NY	No	
27	Citigroup	Michael L. Corbat	CT	New York, NY	No	
28	Comcast	Brian L. Roberts	Philadelphia, PA	Philadelphia, PA	Yes	
29	Pepsico	Indra K. Nooyi	India	Purchase, NY	No	
30	Phillip Morris Int	André Calantzopoulos	Greece	New York, NY	No	
31	Disney	Robert A. Iger	New York, NY	Burbank, CA	No	
32	AbbVie	Richard A. Gonzalez	*Not available*	North Chicago, IL		
33	DowDuPont	Edward D. Breen	Grove City, PA	Midland, MI	No	
34	Merck	Kenneth C. Frazier	Philadelphia	Kenilworth, NJ	No	
35	IBM	Virginia M. Rometty	Chicago, IL	Armonk, NY	No	

Continued…

#	Company	CEO	Hometown	Lives	Yes/No	%
36	Nvidia	Jen-Hsun Huang	Taiwan, China	Santa Clara, CA	No	
37	3M	Inge G. Thulin	Sweden	St. Paul, MN	No	
38	Netflix	Reed Hastings	Boston, MA	Los Gatos, CA	No	
39	McDonald's	Stephen J. Easterbrook	UK	Oak Brook, IL	No	
40	Amgen	Robert A. Bradway	*Not available*	Thousand Oaks, CA		
41	Altria Group	Howard A. Willard III	*Not available*	*Not available*		
42	GE	John L. Flannery Jr.	VA	Boston, MA	No	
43	Honeywell Intl	Darius Adamczyk	Poland	Morris Plains, NJ	No	
44	Nike	Mark G. Parker	Poughkeepsie, NY	Beaverton, OR	No	
45	Adobe Systems	Shantanu Narayen	Hyderabad, India	San Jose, CA	No	
46	Abbott	Miles D. White	Minneapolis, MN	Abbott Park, IL	No	
47	Union Pacific	Lance M. Fritz	*Not available*	Omaha, NE		
48	Bristol-Myers Squibb	Giovanni Caforio	Italy	New York, NY	No	
49	Texas Instruments	Richard K. Templeton	*Not available*	Dallas, TX		
50	United Technologies	Gregory J. Hayes	*Not available*	Farmington, CT		
51	Booking Holdings	Glenn D. Fogel	*Not available*	Norwalk, CT		
52	Gilead Sciences	John F. Milligan IV	*Not available*	Foster City, CA		
53	Morgan Stanley	James P. Gorman	Australia	New York, NY	No	
54	Lockheed Martin	Marillyn A. Hewson	Junction City, KS	Bethesda, Md.	No	
55	GS	Lloyd C. Blankfein	New York, NY	New York, NY	Yes	
56	PayPal	Daniel H. Schulman	NJ	San Jose, CA	No	
57	UPS	David P. Abney	MS	Atlanta, GA	No	
58	Caterpillar	D. James Umpleby III	IN	Deerfield, IL	No	
59	Blackrock	Laurence D. Fink	LA, CA	New York, NY	No	
60	Salesforce.com	Marc R. Benioff	San Francisco, CA	San Fco, CA	Yes	
61	Eli Lilly	David A. Ricks	*Not available*	Indianapolis, IN		
62	US Bancorp	Andrew J. Cecere	*Not available*	Minneapolis, MN		
63	Thermo Fischer Scientific	Marc N. Casper	*Not available*	Waltham, MA		
64	Costco	W. Craig Jelinek	CA	Issaquah, WA	No	
65	Qualcomm	Steven M. Mollenkopf	*Not available*	San Diego, CA		
66	Starbucks	Kevin R. Johnson	Sacramento, CA	Seattle, WA	No	
67	Charter Communications	Thomas M. Rutledge	*Not available*	Stamford, CT		
68	American Express	Stephen J. Squeri	*Not available*	New York, NY		
69	NextEra Energy	James L. Robo	*Not available*	Juno Beach, FL		
70	Kraft Heinz	Bernardo Hees	Brazil	Pittsburgh, PA	No	
71	Time Warner	Jeffrey L. Bewkes	Paterson, NJ	New York, NY	No	
72	Lowe's	Robert A. Niblock	FL	Mooresville, NC	No	
73	PNC Financial Services	William S. Demchak	Pittsburgh, PA	Pittsburgh, PA	Yes	
74	Charles Schwab	Walter W. Bettinger II	Ada, OH	San Francisco, CA	No	
75	ConocoPhillips	Ryan M. Lance	Butte, MT	Houston, TX	No	

Continued…

#	Company	CEO	Hometown	Lives	Yes/No	%
76	Danaher	Thomas P. Joyce Jr.	North Shore, Crystal Lake, IL	Washington DC	No	
77	Twenty-First Century Fox	James R. Murdoch	London, UK	New York, NY	No	
78	Celgene	Mark J. Alles	*Not available*	Summit, NJ		
79	General Dynamics	Phebe N. Novakovic	Pittsburgh, PA	Falls Church, VA	No	
80	Walgreens Boots Alliance	Stefano Pessina	Pescara, Italy	Deerfield, IL	No	
81	FedEx	Frederick W. Smith	Marks, MS	Memphis, TN	No	
82	American Tower	James D. Taiclet Jr.	*Not available*	Boston, MA		
83	CVS Health	Larry J. Merlo	Pittsburgh, PA	Woonsocket, RI	No	
84	Colgate Palmolive	Ian M. Cook	UK	New York, NY	No	
85	Raytheon	Thomas A. Kennedy	*Not available*	Waltham, MA		
86	Mondelez Intl	Dirk Van de Put	Mechelen, Belgium	Deerfield, IL	No	
87	EOG Resources	William R. Thomas	*Not available*	Houston, TX		
88	Northrop Grumman	Wesley G. Bush	WV	Falls Church, VA	No	
89	Micron Technology	Sanjay Mehrotra	Kanpur, India	Boise, ID	No	
90	Stryker	Kevin A. Lobo	Mumbai, India	Kalamazoo, MI	No	
91	Applied Materials	Gary E. Dickerson	*Not available*	Santa Clara, CA		
92	Biogen	Michel Vounatsos	France & Morocco	Cambridge, MA	No	
93	Becton Dickinson	Vincent A. Forlenza	East Orange, NJ	Franklin Lakes, NJ	No	
94	Las Vegas Sands	Sheldon G. Adelson	Boston, MA	Las Vegas, NV	No	
95	Anthem	Gail K. Boudreaux	MA	Indianapolis, IN	No	
96	Aetna	Mark T. Bertolini	Detroit, MI	Hartford, CT	No	
97	Estee Lauder	Fabrizio Freda	Naples, Italy	New York, NY	No	
98	CME Group	Terrence A. Duffy	Chicago, IL	Chicago, IL	Yes	
99	Duke Energy	Lynn J. Good	OH	Charlotte, NC	No	
100	Illinois Tool Works	E. Scott Santi	*Not available*	Glenview, IL		

YES					8	10%
NO					70	90%
TOTAL					78	

APPENDIX B

Where Do the Highest-Paid Actors in the World Live?

Do They Live in Their Hometowns?

Forbes 2017
Highest-Paid Actors
Top 20

#	Actor	Born	Lives	Yes/No	
1	Mark Wahlberg	Dorchester, MA, USA	LA, CA, USA	No	
2	Dwayne Johnson	Hayward, CA, USA	FL, USA	No	
3	Vin Diesel	Alameda County, CA	LA, CA, USA	No	
4	Adam Sandler	Brooklyn, NY, USA	LA, CA, USA	No	
5	Jackie Chan	Hong Kong, China	Hong Kong, China	Yes	
6	Robert Downey Jr.	NYC, USA	Hamptons / Malibu / LA, USA	No	
7	Tom Cruise	Syracuse, NY, USA	LA, CA, USA	No	
8	Shah Rukh Khan	New Delhi, India	Mumbai, India	No	
9	Salman Khan	Indore, India	Mumbai, India	No	
10	Akshay Kumar	Amritsar, India	Mumbai, India	No	
11	Chris Hemsworth	Melbourne, Australia	New South Wales, Australia	No	
12	Tom Hanks	Concord, CA, USA	LA, CA, USA	No	
13	Samuel L. Jackson	Washington DC., USA	LA, CA, USA	No	
14	Ryan Gosling	Ontario, Canada	Los Feliz, CA	No	
15	Ryan Reynolds	Vancouver, Canada	LA, CA, USA	No	
16	Matt Damon	Massachusetts, USA	LA, CA, USA	No	
17	Jeremy Renner	Modesto, CA, USA	LA, CA, USA	No	
18	Chris Evans	Boston, MA, USA	LA, CA, USA	No	
19	Chris Pratt	Minnesota, USA	LA, CA, USA	No	
20	Mark Ruffalo	Wisconsin, USA	NYC, USA	No	
	YES			1	5%
	NO			19	95%
	TOTAL			20	

APPENDIX C

Where Do the Highest-Paid Musicians in the World Live?

Do They Live in Their Hometowns?

Forbes 2017*
Highest-Paid Musicians
Top 25

#	Singer	Born	Lives	Yes/No	%
1	Diddy	New York, NY, USA	Alpine, NJ, USA	No	
2	Beyonce	Houston, TX, USA	New York, NY, USA	No	
3	Drake	Toronto, Canada	Hidden Hills, CA, USA	No	
4	The Weeknd	Toronto, Canada	Hidden Hills, CA, USA	No	
5	Coldplay				
6	Guns N' Roses				
7	Justin Bieber	Ontario, Canada	LA, CA, USA	No	
8	Bruce Springsteen	Long Branch, NJ, USA	Colt Neck, NJ, USA	No	
9	Adele	London, England	London, England	Yes	
10	Metallica				
11	Garth Brooks	Tulsa, OK,USA	Nashville, TN, USA	No	
12	Elton John	Middlesex, England	London, UK / Nice, Fr. / Windsor, UK	No	
13	Paul McCartney	Liverpool, England	Many places, not in Liverpool	No	
14	Red Hot Chili Peppers				
15	Jimmy Buffett	Pescagoula, MS, USA	Palm Beach / Hamptons, USA	No	
16	Calvin Harris	Dumfries, Scotland	LA, CA, USA	No	
17	Taylor Swift	Reading, PA, USA	Nashville / NYC / LA /, USA	No	
18	Kenny Chesney	Knoxville, TN, USA	*Not available*		
19	Luke Bryan	Atlanta, GA, USA	Williamson, TX, USA	No	
20	Celine Dion	Quebec, Canada	Henderson, NV, USA	No	
21	Jay-Z	New York, NY, USA	New York, NY, USA	Yes	
22	Tiesto	Breda, The Netherlands	Several places	No	
23	Bruno Mars	Honolulu, HI, USA	Hollywood, CA, USA	No	
24	The Chainsmokers				
25	J-Lo	New York, NY, USA	New York, NY, USA	Yes	
	YES			**3**	**16%**
	NO			**16**	**84%**
	TOTAL			**19**	

Note: It only consider individual musicians, not musical groups.

NOTE:
Music groups were excluded because each member could live in a different place, so is not
possible to have the data of a group as a whole.

APPENDIX D

Professional Tennis Players (as of July 13, 2018)

Do They Live in Their Hometowns?

Tennis
ATP Worldtour Ranking
As of July 13, 2018.

#	Player	Born	Lives	Yes/No
1	Rafael Nadal	Mallorca, Spain	Mallorca, Spain	Yes
2	Roger Federer	Basel, Switzerland	Wollerau, Switzerland	No
3	Alexander Zverev	Hamburg, Germany	Monaco	No
4	Juan Martin del Potro	Argentina	Argentina	Yes
5	Marin Cilic	Medjugorje, Bosnia-Herzegovina	Monaco	No
6	Grigor Dimitrov	Haskovo, Bulgaria	Monaco	No
7	Dominic Thiem	Wiener Neustadt, Austria	Lichtenwörth, Austria	No
8	Kevin Anderson	Johannesburg, South Africa	Gulf Stream, FL, USA	No
9	David Goffin	Rocourt, Belgium	Monaco	No
10	John Isner	Greensboro, NC, USA	Dallas, TX, USA	No
11	Diego Schwartzman	Buenos Aires, Argentina	Buenos Aires, Argentina	Yes
12	Pablo Carreño Busta	Gijon, Spain	Barcelona, Spain	No
13	Sam Querrey	San Fco, USA	Las Vegas, USA	No
14	Roberto Bautista Agut	Castellon de la Plana, Spain	Castellon de la Plana, Spain	Yes
15	Jack Sock	Lincoln, NE, USA	Kansas City, KS, USA	No
16	Fabio Fognini	Sanremo, Italy	Arma Di Taggia, Italy	No
17	Kyle Edmund	Johannesburg, South Africa	Nassau, Bahamas	No
18	Nick Krygios	Canberra, Australia	Nassau, Bahamas	No
19	Lucas Poille	Grande-Synthe, France	Dubai, UAE	No
20	Borna Coric	Zagreb, Croatia	Dubai, UAE	No
21	Novak Djokovic	Belgrade, Serbia	Monaco	No
22	Hyeon Chung	Suwon, South Korea	Suwon, South Korea	Yes
23	Damir Dzumhur	Sarajevo, Bosnia-Herzegovina	Sarajevo, Bosnia-Herzegovina	Yes
24	Tomas Berdych	Valasske Mezirici, CZE	Monaco	No
25	Denis Shapovalov	Tel Aviv, Israel	Nassau, Bahamas	No
26	Adrian Mannarino	Soisy-Sous-Montmorency, France	Valletta, Malta	No
27	Philipp Kohlschreiber	Augsburg, Germany	Kitzbuhel, Austria	No
28	Kei Nishikori	Shimane, Japan	Bradenton, FL, USA	No
29	Marco Cecchinato	Palermo, Italy	Palermo, Italy	Yes
30	Filip Krajinovic	Sombor, Serbia	Monaco	No
31	Richard Gasquet	Beziers, France	Neuchatel, Switzerland	No
32	Milos Raonic	Podgorica, Montenegro	Monaco	No
33	Andrey Ruvlev	Moscow, Russia	Moscow, Russia	Yes
34	Fernando Verdasco	Madrid, Spain	Doha, Qatar	No
35	Stefanos Tsitsipas	Athens, Greece	Athens, Greece	Yes
YES			**9**	26%
NO			**26**	74%
TOTAL			**35**	

In Monaco	**8**	23%

APPENDIX E

Active F1 Drivers: Where Do They Live?

Formula 1 Drivers
% of drivers that live in their hometown
as of July 2018

#	Driver	Constructor	Born	Lives	Yes/No	%
1	Sebastian Vettel	Ferrari	Happenheim, Germany	Switzerland	No	
2	Lewis Hamilton	Mercedes	Stevenage, England	Monaco	No	
3	Kimi Raikkonen	Ferrari	Espoo, Finland	Switzerland	No	
4	Daniel Ricciardo	Red Bull Racing	Perth, Australia	Monaco	No	
5	Valtteri Bottas	Mercedes	Nastola, Finland	Monaco	No	
6	Max Vestappen	Red Bull Racing	Hasselt, Belgium	Monaco	No	
7	Nico Hulkenberg	Renault	Emmerich am Rhein, Germany	Monaco	No	
8	Fernando Alonso	McLaren	Oviedo, Spain	Dubai	No	
9	Kevin Magnussen	Haas	Roskilde, Denmark	Dubai	No	
10	Carlos Sainz	Renault	Madrid, Spain	London	No	
11	Esteban Ocon	Force India	Evreux, France	Evreux, France	Yes	
12	Sergio Perez	Force India	Guadalajara, México	Switzerland	No	
13	Pierre Gasly	Toro Rosso	Rouen, France	*No information available*		
14	Charles Leclerc	Sauber	Monaco	Monaco	Yes	
15	Romain Grosjean	Haas	Geneva, Switzerland & France	Geneva	Yes	
16	Stoffel Vandoorne	McLaren	Kortrijkt, Belgium	Monaco	No	
17	Lance Stroll	Williams	Montreal, Canada	*No information available*		
18	Marcus Ericsson	Sauber	Kumla, Sweden	*No information available*		
19	Brendon Hartley	Toro Rosso	Palmerston, New Zealand	*No information available*		
20	Sergey Sirotkin	Williams	Moscow, Russia	*No information available*		
	YES				**3**	**20%**
	NO				**12**	**80%**
	TOTAL				**15**	

In Monaco		**7**	**47%**

APPENDIX F

Where Do Professional Golfers Live?

Do They Live in Their Hometowns?

Golf
PGA Ranking
As of July 16, 2018
Top 30

#	Player	Born	Residence	Yes/No
1	Dustin Johnson	Columbia, South Carolina, USA	Palm Beach, FL, USA	No
2	Justin Thomas	Louisville, Kentucky, USA	Goshen, Kentucky, USA	No
3	Bubba Watson	Bagdad, FL, USA	Pensacola, FL, USA	No
4	Justin Rose	Johannesburg, South Africa	Orlando, FL / London, Eng	No
5	Jason Day	Beaudesert, Australia	Forest Lake, Australia	No
6	Bryson DeChambeau	Modesto, CA, USA	Clovis, CA, USA	No
7	Patrick Reed	San Antonio, TX, USA	Spring, TX, USA	No
8	Phil Mickelson	San Diego, CA, USA	Rancho Sta Fe, CA, USA	No
9	Patton Kizzire	Tuscaloosa, Alabama, USA	Sea Island, Georgia, USA	No
10	Tony Finau	Salt Lake City, Utah, USA	Lehi, Utah, USA	No
11	Webb Simpson	Raleigh, North Carolina, USA	Charlotte, North Carolina, USA	No
12	Paul Casey	Cueltenham, England	Phoenix, AZ & Weybridge, England	No
13	Brooks Koepka	West Palm Beach, FL, USA	Jupiter, FL, USA	No
14	Jon Rahm	Barrika, Spain	Scottsdale, AZ, USA	No
15	Patrick Cantlay	Long Beach, CA, USA	Jupiter, FL, USA	No
16	Rickie Fowler	Murrieta, CA, USA	Jupiter, FL, USA	No
17	Chesson Hadley	Raleigh, North Carolina, USA	Raleigh, North Carolina, USA	Yes
18	Kevin Na	Seoul, South Korea	Las Vegas, NV, USA	No
19	Andrew Landry	Port Neches-Groves, TX, USA	Austin, TX, USA	No
20	Marc Leishman	Warrnambool, Australia	Virginia Beach, Virginia, USA	No
21	Brian Harnman	Savannah, Georgia, USA	St Simons Island, Georgia, USA	No
22	Pat Perez	Pheonix, Arizona, USA	Scottsdale, AZ, USA	No
23	Luke List	Seattle, WA, USA	Seal Beach, CA, USA	No
24	Austin Cook	Little Rock, Arkansas, USA	Jonesboro, Arkansas, USA	No
25	Aeron Wise	Cape Town, South Africa	Las Vegas, NV, USA	No
26	Brendan Steele	Idyllwild, CA, USA	Irvine, CA, USA	No
27	Francesco Molinari	Turin, Italy	London, England	No
28	Chez Reavie	Wichita, Kansas, USA	Scottsdale, AZ, USA	No
29	Beau Hossler	Mission Viejo, CA, USA	Austin, TX, USA	No
30	Ryan Armour	Akron, Ohio, USA	Jupiter, FL, USA	No

YES	1	3%
NO	29	97%
TOTAL	30	

APPENDIX G

Top Tennis Players in History with at Least 5 Grand Slam Wins

Where Do They Live after Retirement? Do They Live in Their Hometowns?

Tennis - in History
Grand Slam winners
At least 5 wins in Open Era
As of July 15, 2018

#	Player	# Wins	Born	Residence post-retirement	Yes/No	Comment
1	Roger Federer	20				Still playing
2	Rafael Nadal	17				Still playing
3	Pete Sampras	14	Washington DC, USA	Lake Sherwood, California, USA	No	
4	Novak Djokovic	13				Still playing
5	Bjorn Borg	11	Stockholm, Sweden	Monaco	No	
6	Jimmy Connors	8	East St. Louis, Illinois, USA	Santa Barbara, Califronia, USA	No	
7	Ivan Lendl	8	Ostrava, Czechoslovakia	Goshen, CT., USA & Vero Beach, FL, USA	No	
8	Andre Agassi	8	Las Vegas, NV, USA	Las Vegas, NV, USA	Yes	
9	John McEnroe	7	NYC, USA*	NYC, USA	Yes	
10	Mats Wilander	7	Vaxjo, Sweden	Hailey, Idaho, USA	No	
11	Stefan Edberg	6	Vastervik, Sweden	London, England	No	
12	Boris Becker	6	Leimen, Germany	Schwyz, Switzerland	No	
13	Rod Laver	5	Rockhampton, Queensland, AU	Carlsbad, California, USA	No	
14	John Newcombe	5	Sydney, Australia	Sydney, Australia	Yes	
	YES				3	27%
	NO				8	73%
	TOTAL				11	

* Born in Germany and after 1 year to NYC

APPENDIX H

Where Do Top Retired Golfers (with at least 6 "Majors" Wins) Live?

Do They Live in Their Hometowns?

Golf - in History
Majors winners in history
At least 6 wins
As of July 2018

#	Player	# Wins	Born	Residence post-retirement	Yes/No	Comment
1	Jack Nicklaus	18	Columbus, Ohio, USA	Palm Beach, FL, USA	No	
2	Tiger Woods	14				Still playing
3	Walter Hagen	11	Rochester, New York, USA	Traverse City, Michigan	No	
4	Ben Hogan	9	Stephenville, TX, USA	Forth Worth, TX, USA	No	
5	Gary Player	9	Johannesburg, South Africa	Jupiter Island, FL, USA & Colesberg, SA	No	
6	Tom Watson	8	Kansas City, Missouri	Stillwell, Kansas	No	
7	Sam Snead	7	Ashwood, Virginia, USA	Hot Springs, Virginia, USA	Yes	
8	Arnold Palmer	7	Latrobe, Pennsylvania, USA	Latrobe & Orlando & La Quinta Calif.	Yes	
9	Gene Sarazen	7	New York, USA	Naples, FL, USA	No	
10	Bobby Jones	7	Atlanta, Georgia, USA	Atlanta, Georgia, USA	Yes	
11	Harry Vardon	7	Channel Islands, Britain	Whetstone, London, UK	No	
12	Lee Trevino	6	Dallas, TX, USA	Dallas, TX, USA	Yes	
13	Nick Faldo	6	Welwyn Garden City, England	Orlando, FL, USA	No	
	YES				4	33%
	NO				8	67%
	TOTAL				12	

APPENDIX I

Formula 1 Drivers: Where do they live after retirement?

(The list includes the drivers in history who have at least 2 championship win.)

F1 - in History
Championship Winners
At least 2 wins

#	Driver	# Wins	Born	Residence post-retirement	Yes/No	Comment
1	Michael Schumacher	7	Hürth, Germany	Gland, Switzerland	No	
2	Juan Manuel Fangio	5	Buenos Aires / ARG	Buenos Aires / ARG	Yes	
3	Alain Prost	4	Lorette, France	Nyon, Switzerland	No	
4	- Lewis Hamilton -	4				Still racing
5	- Sebastian Vettel -	4				Still racing
6	Jack Barbham	3	Hurtsville, Australia	Gold Coast, Australia	No	
7	Jackie Stewart	3	Milton, Scotland	Begnins, Switzerland, now Ellesborough, England.	No	
8	Niki Lauda	3	Vienna, Austria	*No information available*		
9	Nelson Piquet	3	Rio de Janeiro, Brazil	*No information available*		
10	- Ayrton Senna -	3				Died before retirement
11	- Alberto Ascari -	2				Died before retirement
12	Graham Hill	2	London, England	Hertfordshire, England	Yes	
13	- Jim Clark -	2				Died before retirement
14	Emerson Fittipaldi	2	Sao Paulo, Brazil	Miami, FL, USA.	No	
15	Mika Hakkinen	2	Vantaa, Finland	Thurgau, Switzerland	No	
16	- Fernando Alonso -	2				Still racing
	YES				2	25%
	NO				6	75%
	TOTAL				8	

APPENDIX J

TVM (The time value of money)
US$

		Payment			How much it will be in the following years:					House cleaner + cappuccino + cigarettes + 2 children
	Initial Investment	Daily	Monthly	Yearly	5	18	20	30	50	
1 Gym membership			120.00		8,591					
2 House cleaner		18.06	541.67	6,500.00			282,170	660,822		
3 Tall Cappuccino		2.75	82.50				42,976	100,648		
4 Home-made coffee**		0.40	12.00				**6,251**	**14,640**		
5 Cigarettes		7.00	210.00				109,395	256,194		
6 Child #1		35.96	1,078.70 *			464,620				
7 Child #2		35.96	1,078.70 *			464,620				
8 Makeup		1.50	45.00						245,163	
TOTAL						929,241	434,541			**1,363,782**
Coffee difference between Starbucks and homemade							36,725	86,008		

*The $1,078.70 is the $233,000 (the cost of a child for 18 years) divided by 216 months.

** Home made coffee is not considered in the total amount.

APPENDIX K

TVM (The time value of money)
US$

RATE   7%

	Payment				How much it will be in the following years:				
	Initial Investment				Year 5				
Home gym	4,000		94.51		5,671				

APPENDIX L

Life Expectancy – OECD Countries

OECD Countries	Life Expectancy* In years		OECD Countries	Life Expectancy* In years
Members			**Adherents**	
1 Australia	82	37	Argentina	77
2 Austria	82	38	Brazil	74
3 Belgium	81	39	Colombia	76
4 Canada	82	40	Costa Rica	79
5 Chile	79	41	Egypt	73
6 Czech Republic	79	42	Jordan	75
7 Denmark	80	43	Kazakhstan	71
8 Estonia	77	44	Morocco	77
9 Finland	81	45	Peru	74
10 France	82	46	Romania	75
11 Germany	81	47	Ukrain	72
12 Greece	81			
13 Hungary	76			
14 Iceland	83			
15 Ireland	81			
16 Israel	83			
17 Italy	82			
18 Japan	85			
19 Korea	83			
20 Latvia	75			
21 Lithuania	75			
22 Luxembourg	82			
23 Mexico	76			
24 Netherlands	81			
25 New Zealand	81			
26 Norway	82			
27 Poland	78			
28 Portugal	79			
29 Slovak Republic	77			
30 Slovenia	78			
31 Spain	82			
32 Sweden	82			
33 Switzerland	83			
34 Turkey	75			
35 United Kingdom	81			
36 United States	80			

AVERAGE 79

APPENDIX M

Hours Worked–2017–OECD Countries
Annual Average
https://data.oecd.org/emp/hours-worked.htm

Continued...

	COUNTRY	HOURS WORKED ANNUAL HOURS		COUNTRY	HOURS WORKED ANNUAL HOURS
1	Germany	1,356	21	Hungary	1,740
2	Denmark	1,408	22	New Zealand	1,753
3	Norway	1,419		**OECD TOTAL**	**1,759**
4	Netherlands	1,433	23	Czech Republic	1,776
5	France	1,514	24	United States	1,780
6	Luxembourg	1,518	25	Turkey	1,832
7	Belgium	1,546	26	Lithuania	1,844
8	Switzerland	1,570	27	Estonia	1,857
9	Sweden	1,609	28	Portugal	1,863
10	Austria	1,613	29	Latvia	1,875
11	Finland	1,628	30	Israel	1,885
12	Slovenia	1,655	31	Poland	1,895
13	Australia	1,676	32	Chile	1,954
14	United Kingd	1,681	33	Russia	1,980
15	Spain	1,687	34	Greece	2,018
16	Canada	1,695	35	Korea	2,024
17	Japan	1,710	36	Costa Rica	2,179
18	Slovak Repuʟ	1,714	37	Mexico	2,257
19	Italy	1,723			
20	Ireland	1,738			

APPENDIX N

Working period (25 to 60 years old)

PERIOD		FORMULA			#1 Germany	AVG OECD	#37 Mexico	#24 USA
A			# Years	35	35	35	35	35
B			Days/year	365				
C			Weekends	104				
D			Vacations	20				
E			Holidays	10				
F	a Year	=B-C-D-E	#Working days	231				
G	a Year	=B-F	# Nonworking days	134				
H	a Year	=Fx8	#Working hours	1,848	1,356	1,759	2,257	1,780
I	a Year	=(Gx24)+(Fx16)	#Nonworking hours	6,912	7,404	7,001	6,503	6,980
J	Working years	=HxA	#Working hours	64,680	47,460	61,565	78,995	62,300
K	Working years	=IxA	#Nonworking hours	241,920	259,140	245,035	227,605	244,300

*OECD Countries - 2017**

Nonworking period (60 to 79 years old)

PERIOD		FORMULA			Germany	OECD	Mexico	USA
A			# Years	19	19	19	19	19
B			Days/year	365	365	365	365	365
C			Weekends					
D			Vacations					
E			Holidays					
F	a Year	=B-C-D-E	#Working days					
G	a Year	=B-F	# Nonworking days	365	365	365	365	365
H	a Year	=Fx8	#Working hours					
I	a Year	=Gx24	#Nonworking hours	8,760	8,760	8,760	8,760	8,760
J	Nonworking years	=HxA	#Working hours	-				
K	Nonworking years	=IxA	#Nonworking hours	166,440	166,440	166,440	166,440	166,440

	#1		AVG		#37		#24	
Total working hours	64,680	14%	47,460	10%	61,565	13%	78,995	17%	62,300	13%
Total nonworking hours	408,360	86%	425,580	90%	411,475	87%	394,045	83%	410,740	87%
Total Hours	473,040		473,040		473,040		473,040		473,040	

*https://data.oecd.org/emp/hours-worked.htm

ABOUT THE AUTHOR

Pablo Ponce has been working for big corporations in the consumer goods and pharmaceutical sectors, assuming marketing and sales positions. He has an MBA from IE Business School in Madrid, Spain.

He writes nonfiction: psychology, a theme he's constantly investigating. He's passionate about a healthy lifestyle.

NOTES

[1]Satoshi Kanazawa and Norman P.Li. "The Savanna Theory of Happiness," in *The Oxford Handbook of Evolution, Biology and Society*, ed Rosemary L. Hopcroft (Oxford: Oxford University Press 2018), 171-94.

[2] Kanazawa and Li. 171-94.

[3] Merriam-Webster.

[4] Sleep.org

[5] Daniel H. Pink. *When* (New York: Riverhead Books, 2017).

[6] Investopedia, by Stephanie Loiacono, Updated November 30,2017.

[7] Malcom Gladwell, *Outliers* (New York: Little Brown & Company, 2008).

[8] Frans Johansson. *The Click Moment* (New York: Penguin Group 2012).

[9] C. Claiborne Ray, "Brain Power," *New York Times*, September 1, 2008. https://www.nytimes.com/2008/09/02/science/02qna.html.

[10] Gallup statistics. March 2004.

[11] Tom W, Smith, Michael Hout, and Peter V. Marsden. General Social Surveys, 1972–2014:
Cumulative Codebook. (Chicago: National Opinion Research Center, 2015).

[12] Meliksah Demir. Haley Orthel, and Adrian Keith Andelin, "Friendship and Happiness," in *The Oxford Handbook of Happiness*, eds Susan A. David, Ilona Boniwell, and Amanda Conley Ayres (Oxford: Oxford University Press, 2013) 860-70; Meliksah Demir, Haley Orthel-Clark, Metin Özdemir and Sevgi Bayram Özdemir, "Friendship and Happiness Among Young Adults," in *Frindship and Happiness*: Across *The Life-Span and Cultures*, ed. Maliksah Demir (Dordrecht, the Netherlands: Springer, 2015), 117–35.

[13] Robin Dunbar, "Can the Internet Buy You More Friends?" *TEDxObserver,* from the segment "Is There A Limit to

How Many Friends We Can Have?" *TED Radio Hour*, January 13, 2017, https://www.npr.org/2017/01/13/509358157/is-there-a-limit-to-how-many-friends-we-can-have.

[14] R.I.M. Dunbar, "Neocortex Size as a Constraint on Group Size Primates," *Journal of Human Evolution* 22. No 6. (June 1992) 469-93.

[15] CNN Money January 9, 2017

[16] CNN Money January 9, 2017

[17] Data Worldbank.org.

[18] Anthony Shorrocks, Jim Davies, and Rodrigo Lluberas, *Credit Suisse Global Wealth Report 2017*. (Zurich: Credit Suisse Research Institute, 2017).

[19] *Parenthood*, directed by Ron Howard, written by Lowell Ganz, Babaloo Mandel and Ron Howard, 1989.

[20] Michael Gioia "Stanford's admission rate drops to 4.69%," *The Stanford Daily*, March 25, 2016, https://www.stanforddaily.com/2016/03/25/stanfords-admission-rate-drops-to-4-69/.

[21] "Record Number of Americans Apply to #BeAnAstronaut at Nasa," Nasa.gov, February 19'2016, https://www.nasa.gov/press-release/record-number-of-americans-apply-to-beanastronaut-at-nasa.

[22] Guy Trebay, "Angels in Stripper Heels," *New York Times*, November 3, 2010, https://www.nytimes.com/2010/11/04/fashion/04Gimlet.html.

[23] National Center for Education Statistics

[24] 5 Most Addictive Drugs, American Addiction Centers, updated February 15, 2019, https://americanaddictioncenters.org/adult-addiction-treatment-programs/most-addictive.

[25] Carl L. Hart, Joanne Csete, and Don Habibi, *Methamphetamine: Fact vs. Fiction and Lessons from the Crack Hysteria*," (New York: Department of Psychology, Columbia University, 2014).

[26] Gladwell, *Outliers*.

[27] Expat Insider 2017.

[28] This data is not perfectly calculated because the data for expats in the world is of 2017 and the people who are employed in the world is as of 2011. It is not exact but to give you an idea.

[29] "Global employment: What is the World Employment Rate?" *The Guardian,* 2011.

https://www.theguardian.com/news/datablog/2011/jan/25/global-economy-globalrecession.

[30] J. Glass, R.W. Simon, and M.A. Anderson, "Parenthood and Happiness: Effects of Work-Family Reconciliation Policies in 22 OECD Countries," *American Journal of Sociology* 122, no.3 (November 2016): 886-929, doi: 10.1086/688892.

[31] May Bulman, "Newlyweds more likely to gain weight, scientist find," *Independent*, December 3, 2017, https://www.independent.co.uk/news/health/newly-weds-more-likely-gain-weight-scientists-glasgow-university-a8089211.html.

[32] Craig F. Garfield, Greg Duncan, Anna Gutina, Joshua Rutsohn, Thomas W. McDade, Emma K. Adam, Rebekah Levine Coley, P. Lindsay Chase-Lansdale, "Longitudinal Study of Body Mass Index in Young Males and the Transition to Fatherhood," *American Journal of Men's Health*, July 21, 2015, https://doi.org/10.1177/1557988315596224.

[33] Civic science platform

[34] George E. Vaillant, *Triumphs of Experience: The Men of the Harvard Grant Study*. (Cambridge, MA: Belknap Press, 2015).

[35] Matthew D. Johnson. "Having children? Here's how kids ruin your romantic relationship," *The Conversation*, https://theconversation.com/have-children-heres-how-kids-ruin-your-romantic-relationship-57944, May 6, 2016.

[36] Arild S. Foss, "Older people just as happy without children," *ScienceNordic*, November 24, 2012, http://sciencenordic.com/older-people-just-happy-without-children.

[37] Pete Pfitzinger, and Scott Douglas, *Advanced Marathoning*. 2nd. ed. (Champaign, IL: Human Kinetics, 2008).

[38] Alex Lickerman, "The meaning of true friendship: What is it that makes a good friend?" *Psychology Today blog*. December 15, 2013. https://www.psychologytoday.com/us/blog/happiness-in-world/201312/the-true-meaning-friendship.

[39] Niall McCarthy, "The Countries with the Most Native-Born People Living Overseas," Forbes, January 15, 2016, https://www.forbes.com/sites/niallmccarthy/2016/01/15/the-countries-with-the-most-native-born-people-living-abroad-infographic/#799a6c137924

[40] "Expat Insider 2017." InterNations, www.internations.org/expat-insider.

[41] "Expat Insider 2017."

[42] "Expat Insider 2017."

[43] "Expat Insider 2017."

[44] *Fortune* 500 list. Companies ordered by market cap as of March 29, 2018.

[45] *Forbes* 2017. Top-20 highest-paid actors.

[46] *Forbes* 2017. Top-25 highest-paid musicians.

[47] ATP World Tour ranking singles as of July 12, 2018.

[48] List of Formula 1 drivers, 2018 championship.

[49] Top 30 PGA ranking as of July 16, 2018.

[50] "The average career of a tennis player ranked in the Top ten is 16 +-3,8 years for men and 15.8 +-4.4 for women," M. Guillaume, S. Lens, M.Tafflet, L. Quinquis, B. Montalvan, K. Schaal, H. Nassif, F.D. Desgorces, and J.F. Toussaint. "Success and Decline: Top 10 Players Follow a Biphasic Course," *Medicine & Science in Sports and Exercise* 43, no 11. (November 2011):2148-54.

[51] All male tennis players who had won at least five Grand Slams in open era as of July 15, 2018.

[52] Top 100 PGA Ranking as of July 23, 2018.

[53] All male golfers who had won at least six majors as of July 15, 2018.

[54] John F. Helliwell, Richard Layard and Jeffrey Sachs eds., *World Happiness Report 2017*. (New York: United Nations Sustainable Development Solutions Network, 2017).

[55] www.gov.uk. Tier 1 (investor) visa. July 24, 2018.

[56] Benjamin Graham. *The Intelligent Investor*. (New York: Harper & Brothers, 1949).

[57] "The States of the Nation's Housing 2018," *Joint Center for Housing Studies of Harvard University*, (2018): 30, https://www.jchs.harvard.edu/sites/default/files/Harvard_JCHS_State_of_the_Nations_Housing_2018.pdf.

[58] Chase Peterson-Withorn, "Forbes Billionaires: Full List of the 500 Richest People in the World 2015," *Forbes*, March 2, 2015, https://www.forbes.com/sites/chasewithorn/2015/03/02/forbes-billionaires-full-list-of-the-500-richest-people-in-the-world-2015/#1e7564b645b9.

[59] Janet Lowe, Google Speaks: Secrets of the World's Greatest Billionaire Entrepreneurs. Sergey Brin and Larry Page (Hoboken, NJ: John Wiley and Sons, 2009).

[60] Matt Mansfield, "Startup Statistics – The Numbers you Need to Know," "Of all small businesses started in 2014, 56 percent made it to the fifth year (2018)" *Small Business Trends*, March 28,

2019, https://smallbiztrends.com/2019/03/startup-statistics-small-business.html.

[61] Daniel M. Blumenthal and Mark S. Gold, "Neurobiology of Food Addiction," Harvard Medical School and Harvard Business School, Harvard University. DOI: 10.1097/MCO.0b013e32833ad4d4, July 2010.

[62] Phillippa Lally, Cornelia H.M. van Jaarsveld, Henry W.W. Potts, and Jane Wardle, "How habits are formed: Modelling habit formation in the real world," *European Journal of Social Psychology* 40, no. 6 (October 2010): 998-1009.

[63] Maxwell Maltz, *Psycho-Cybernetics* (New York: Simon & Schuster, 1960).

[64] William Lowndes (1652-1724 Former Secretary to the Treasury of Great Britain), he used nearly identical language but used British currency: "Take care of the pence and the pounds will take care of themselves." That's the origin of the saying wrongly attributed to Benjamin Franklin using US currency.

[65] Shorrocks, Davies, and Lluberas, Credit Suisse Global Wealth Report 2017.

[66] Shorrocks, Davies, and Lluberas, Credit Suisse Global Wealth Report 2017. These two graphics were used with permission of Anthony Shorrocks, one of the authors and Stephanie Lüdin of Credit Suisse.

[67] Thomas J. Stanley and William D. Danko, *The Millionaire Next Door: The Surprising Secrets of America's Wealthy*, (Lanham, MD: Taylor Trade Publishing, 1996).

[68] "Grape expectations: Is red wine good for your heart?" *Harvard Health Publishing*. Harvard Medical School, last revised February 2018. https://www.health.harvard.edu/heart-health/grape-expectations-is-red-wine-good-for-your-heart

[69] "What is the Average Annual Return for the S&P 500?" Investopedia, last revised May 2018.

[70] "A 130,7 Bn Cosmetic Skin Market 2017: Global Industry Analysis, Trends, Market Size and Forecasts to 2023 – Research and Markets," Business Wire, last revised September 27, 2017, https://www.businesswire.com/news/home/20170927005526/en/130.7-Bn-Cosmetic-Skin-Care-Market-2017.

[71] Sissi Johnson, "How much is your face worth? American Woman Wverage at $8 per Day" Huffington Post, last revised March 8, 2017, https://www.huffingtonpost.com/entry/how-much-

is-your-face-worth-american-women-
average_us_58befa65e4b06660f479e594.

[72] Alex L. Jones, Robin S.S. Kramer, and Robert Ward, "Miscalibrations in Judgements of Attractiveness with Cosmetics," *Quarterly Journal of Experimental Psychology* 67, no. 10 (October 1, 2014): 2060-2068.

[73] *Fortune* 500 Global, 2018.

[74] "The States of the Nation's Housing 2018," *Joint Center for Housing Studies of Harvard University*, (2018): 30, https://www.jchs.harvard.edu/sites/default/files/Harvard_JCHS_Stat e_of_the_Nations_Housing_2018.pdf.

[75] Jennifer Pearlman, "Is gaining weight inevitable as we age?" *The Globe and Mail*, May 11, 2018, https://www.theglobeandmail.com/life/health-and-fitness/health-advisor/is-gaining-weight-inevitable-as-we-age/article19490838/.

[76] Gallup 2017.

[77] LinkedIn. 2016.

[78] Stanley and Danko, *The Millionaire Next Door*, 131.

[79] *The Wall Street Journal*. March 2, 2016.

[80] Eckhart Tolle, *The Power of Now: A Guide to Spiritual Enlightenment*, (Novato, CA: New World Library,1999).

[81] World Health Organization. 2015

[82] World Health Organization. 2015.

[83] Sarah Berger, "Jeff Bezos gave away more money than Bill Gates , Mark Zuckerberg combined in 2018," *CNBC*, February 13, 2019, https://www.cnbc.com/2019/02/13/philanthropy-50-how-much-bezos-gates-zuckerberg-charities-gave-away.html

[84] Stanley and Danko, *The Millionaire Next Door*, 131.

[85] Mary Ann Emanuele, and Nicholas Emanuele, "Alcohol and the Male Reproductive System," *National Institute of Alcohol Abuse and Alcoholism*, https://pubs.niaaa.nih.gov/publications/arh25-4/282-287.htm.

[86] Anna Almendrala, "Alcohol Companies Are Funding Research to Convince You Drinking is Healthy," Huffpost, last revised April 17, 2018. https://www.huffingtonpost.com/entry/alcohol-companies-want-you-to-drink-more-and-theyre-funding-research-to-make-it-happen_us_5ad123bce4b077c89ce8a835.

[87] Adam Grant, "Finding the Hidden Value in Your Network," *LinkedIn*, June 17, 2013, https://www.linkedin.com/pulse/20130617112202-69244073-finding-the-hidden-value-in-your-network/.

[88] Merriam-Webster.

[89] Glass, Simon and Anderson "Parenthood and Happiness."

[90] Julia Poncela-Casasnovas, Mario Gutiérrez-Roig, Carlos Gracia-Lázaro, Julian Vicens, Jesús Gómez-Gardeñes, Josep Perelló, Yamir Moreno, Jordi Duch, and Ángel Sánchez. "Humans Display a Reduced Set of Consistent Behavioral Phenotypes in Dyadic Games," *Science Advances* 2, no. 8 (August 2016) Vol. 2, no. 8, e1600451. DOI: 10.1126/sciadv.1600451. http://hdl.handle.net/10016/23598.

[91] Jamin Halberstadt, Joshua Conrad Jackson, David Bilkey, Jonathan Jong, Harvey Whitehouse, Craig McNaughto, Stefanie Zollmann, "Incipient Social Groups: An Analysis via In-Vivo Behavioral Tracking," PLOS.org, March 23, 2016, https://doi.org/10.1371/journal.pone.0149880.

[92] Seth Meyers "7 Reasons Why We Envy Our Friends (or Vice Versa)," *Psychology Today blog*, July 8, 2015. https://www.psychologytoday.com/us/blog/insight-is-2020/201507/7-reasons-why-we-envy-our-friends-and-vice-versa.

[93] Adam M. Grant, "Rethinking the Extraverted Sales Ideal: The Ambivert advantage," *Psychological Science* 24, no. 6 (June 1, 2013): 1024–30, https://doi.org/10.1177%2F0956797612463706.

[94] Richard A. Lippa, "The preferred traits of mates in a cross-national study of heterosexual and homosexual men and women: an examination of biological and cultural influences." *National Center of Biotechnology Information (NCBI)*. https://www.ncbi.nlm.nih.gov/pubmed/17380374, April 2007.

[95] "Study in STIs," World Health Organization, 2015.

[96] Ned Herrmann, "Is it true that the creativity resides in the right side of the brain?" Scientific American, https://www.scientificamerican.com/article/is-it-true-that-creativit/.

[97] John Tierney, "What is Nostalgia Good For? Quite a Bit, Research Shows," *New York Times,* July 8, 2013, https://www.nytimes.com/2013/07/09/science/what-is-nostalgia-good-for-quite-a-bit-research-shows.html.

[98] Tierney, "What is Nostalgia Good For?"

[99] "Hermann Ebbinghaus' self-measured forgetting curve," The Atlas, https://www.theatlas.com/charts/H16nE-jvM.

[100] Walter Isaacson, *Leonardo Da Vinci*, (New York: Simon & Schuster, 2017).

---

[101] "Donor Recruitment," California Cryobank, https://www.cryobank.com/how-it-works/donor-recruitment/.

[102] Samantha Pearson, "Demand for American Sperm is Skyrocketing in Brazil," *The Wall Street Journal*, last revised March 22, 2018, https://www.wsj.com/articles/in-mixed-race-brazil-sperm-imports-from-u-s-whites-are-booming-1521711000.

[103] Pearson, "Demand for American Sperm is Skyrocketing in Brazil."

[104] "Men who are interested in becoming applicants must be between 18-39 years of age, healthy and have no other significant risk factors. Of those who originally apply, less than 1% of applicants are accepted as sperm donors for Fairfax Cryobank, indicative of our intensely rigorous screening processes." Fairfax Cryobank, https://fairfaxcryobank.com/about-our-donors.

[105] OECD Countries list, http://www.oecd.org/about/membersandpartners/list-oecd-member-countries.htm, and "The World Factbook," Central Intelligence Agency, https://www.cia.gov/library/publications/the-world-factbook/rankorder/2102rank.html.

[106] OECD Countries 2017, https://data.oecd.org/emp/hours-worked.htm.